POLICE
SOCIAL WORK

POLICE SOCIAL WORK

By

EDWARD M. COLBACH, M.D.

Former Director
Multnomah County Law Enforcement Counseling Program
Associate Clinical Professor of Psychiatry
University of Oregon Medical School
Portland, Oregon

and

CHARLES D. FOSTERLING, M.S.W., M.P.H.

Director
Law Enforcement Counseling and Involuntary Commitment Programs
Multnomah County, Oregon

CHARLES C THOMAS • PUBLISHER
Springfield • *Illinois* • *U.S.A.*

Published and Distributed Throughout the World by

CHARLES C THOMAS • PUBLISHER

Bannerstone House

301-327 East Lawrence Avenue, Springfield, Illinois, U.S.A.

© *1976, by* CHARLES C THOMAS • PUBLISHER

ISBN 0-398-03505-9

Library of Congress Catalog Card Number: 75-37909

Printed in the United States of America
R-1

Library of Congress Cataloging in Publication Data

Colbach, Edward M
  Police social work.

  Bibliography: p.
  Includes index.
    1. Police social work.   I. Fosterling, Charles D.,
joint author.   II. Title.
HV8079.2.C64   363.2'3   75-37909
ISBN 0-398-03505-9

to our officer friends who serve at
all hours under all circumstances

CONTENTS

POLICE
SOCIAL WORK

INTRODUCTION

THE following situation is true, with enough changes to disguise the people involved. It is a good vehicle in which to convey some of the main ideas of this book.

Stephen Stone lived with his wife and two young children in a middle class neighborhood on the outskirts of Portland, Oregon. He was thirty-five years old, and his wife, Mary, was thirty-three. They had been married for eight years. It was the first marriage for both. Their son, John, was seven, and their daughter, Sue, was four.

Stephen worked as a truck driver for a local produce company. He had had this job for two years, about the average amount of time he held any job before relations between him and his employer became too strained for him to continue. He also attended a nearby community college three nights a week, taking courses which prepared him for a job as a veterinarian's assistant. Stephen had always preferred animals to people.

His wife did not work. She liked to think of herself as an old-fashioned housewife, devoting herself mainly to her husband and her children. The family did not have many close friends and tended to remain somewhat isolated. Most of their activities centered around the home.

In many ways they appeared no different than numerous other young American families in the same socioeconomic situation. But there really was a difference.

Perhaps due to some hereditary defect, or perhaps due to problems in his own early parenting, Stephen tended to perceive life a bit differently than his neighbors or his coworkers. It was a small difference, but it was a definite one, and in many ways it made him a very tortured individual.

If a neighbor's barking dog awakened him at night, for example, it aroused intense anger in him. He had a strong suspicion that this somehow represented a purposeful violation of his sleep. When his car had a flat tire one morning, he wondered if maybe a neighbor who did not like him had done it. When little John was punched in the eye by a neighbor child, Stephen saw it as just another example of others harassing him and his family. He was not sure of the reasons for all of this. He suspected it might have something to do with his religion, or his nationality, or his looks, or the fact that he drove a newer car. While the "why" of it all was unclear, he was sure that he was viewed as an enemy in his own neighborhood. As a result, he became rather distant from, even hostile to, his neighbors. They reacted in kind, thereby further proving his point. At work it was more of the same. He had almost been fired from his current job a number of times because of disagreements with his superior. His boss wanted things done a certain way, but Stephen was certain that he knew a better way. He could never convince his boss of this, a fact that Stephen attributed to his supervisor's personality inadequacies. He had been passed over for a minor promotion, and he was convinced that this was because he was unfairly misunderstood. He wondered whether some of his coworkers had told some lies about him, and he, therefore, kept an appropriate distance from them. The other drivers often hung together, telling jokes. He never thought the jokes were as funny as the others did, and he wondered whether some of their laughing was directed at him. And the more he expected the others to shut him out of their circle, the more it happened, thus fulfilling his own prophecy.

This whole situation was nothing new to Stephen. Generally, things had been that way throughout most of his life. With the pressures of making a living and raising a family, however, they did seem to be getting a bit worse. Often he did not sleep well at night, he occasionally did not feel like eating, and he was aware of a constant tenseness, a constant need to be on guard.

His wife was a rather passive person who took strength in her husband's rigid belief that he saw things more clearly than others. She stood behind him in all things, never questioning his interpretation of events. If she did question, of course, he would not have been able to tolerate marriage with her.

The children had their natural tendency to reach out to the world, to explore and to experiment. They sensed their father's fear of an apparently alien world, however, and they too were becoming more cautious, more likely to see the hidden evil motives in even minor misfortunes like a lost toy.

To use a technical term, Stephen Stone had a strong tendency toward *paranoid thinking*. He was an extremely angry person who could not easily recognize or accept this aspect of himself. So instead, he attributed this anger not to himself but to others by use of the unconscious defense mechanisms of projection. It was not *he* who was angry and vicious, it was *them*. *They* were the enemies.

He had never had any kind of mental breakdown, but life in general was extremely difficult for him. The constant need to be on guard took its toll in many ways. And the more he expected the attack, the more he tried to defend against it by distance and hostility, the more an actual attack came. So he had a continuing supply of data to prove that others really did not like him and were out to hurt him. He could see no point in ever seeking professional help for his affliction, since it was not his problem but the problem of the others who were mean and petty and insensitive and unfair.

To use another technical term, Stephen might be diagnosed as having a *paranoid personality*. The world has more than its share of such people, and they are often at the center of a variety of complicated problems.

Stephen's particular situation was approaching a bit of a crisis. He prided himself on the neat landscaping around his modest home. He kept the grass closely cut, pulled every weed, and trimmed the edges regularly. The view out of his front window seemed always to be ruined, however, by a particular neighbor who parked his second car right in front of Stephen's house. Stephen kept his own car in the garage as much as possible, and bitterly resented his landscape being spoiled.

Through the summer months Stephen took this silently but seethed inside. He made a few offhand remarks to the neighbor's children, and once even told the neighbor that cars parked on the street "cluttered up a neighborhood." But still the car was parked there with regularity. Stephen believed that this was being done just to spite him. Finally, he could take it no more. About 6:30 P.M. one Friday evening the neighbor arrived home from work and parked in his usual place. Stephen ran out to meet him and vehemently told him to move the car or he would "kick the windshield in." The neighbor pointed out that it was a public street, and he could park anywhere he pleased. If Stephen kicked his car in he would kick Stephen's face in. The verbal threats loudly escalated, and each man shoved the other, the neighbor shoving Stephen first. Other people came to their windows to see what was going on, as did Mary and the children. When the children asked what was happening, Mary tearfully told them that their "mean neighbor was trying to hurt Daddy."

One of the neutral onlookers became frightened that someone would get hurt and called the police. The caller was excited enough so that the police dispatcher could not determine exactly what was going on. He did get the location and the information that there was some sort of neighborhood disturbance where at least two men were fighting in the street and threatening to kill each other. He gave the call to his nearest patrol car and dispatched a second car as cover, since the situation sounded potentially explosive.

Robin Wells was the first officer to receive the call. He was thirty-one years old and had been a policeman for about five years. He had a high school education and had been a department store salesman before joining the force. He had joined mainly for economic reasons. He also wanted a job that was less confining and that gave him more of an opportunity to move about. There was some idealism in his decision in that he had definite ideas that his beloved America was somehow being destroyed by vague liberal forces. He hoped to help reverse this trend.

He had been disillusioned during his time on the force. Economically he was still better off than he had been. But in many ways his new job was just as confining as his old one. Physically he moved about more, but he often felt overwhelmed by all the restrictions placed on him. Strict dress and conduct codes that seemed to overemphasize the public servant aspect of his job annoyed him. Always he was expected to look, talk and act in a professional manner, even in the face of abuse from others. He wanted to catch criminals, not be a social worker. Yet, most of what he was called upon to do seemed like social work. What did he care about black culture? Yet, he was being asked to learn about it, so that he would properly relate to the few blacks in his district. And what about alcoholism? Public intoxication was no longer a crime, so he was now expected to decide upon some other disposition than jail for the drunks he encountered.

But probably his biggest disillusionment came when he occasionally apprehended a burglar or a mugger or some other real lawbreaker. Then the rest of the criminal justice system usually let him down. Either the judges were too lenient in sentencing or the parole board was too quick to release. The liberal takeover was even worse than he had anticipated. He had thought about changing jobs once again, but there was really nothing else he knew how to do. So he had decided to stick it out until retirement.

When Robin received the neighborhood disturbance call this evening, he could almost feel his blood pressure rising. He did not consider such calls real police work. Usually they involved alcohol and emotionally unstable people who needed a psychiatrist or a social worker rather than a policeman. But where do you get a psychiatrist or a social worker to make a house call on a Friday evening? He had no training in psychology, except for a very inadequate course in the police academy five years ago.

As he approached the address, he could see two red faced men shouting and gesturing vehemently at each other in the street. He felt a surge of fear, but then this was overwhelmed by a strong awareness of contempt. The "jerks," who represented a general citizenry he thought less of daily, were at it again. He would have to play the sweet, polite mediator. If only the police had a free hand. A quick club to the head and jail would solve this situation immediately. He had heard stories from older officers. But that was a different era in police work.

As he parked his car Robin tried hard to put his hostility aside. He was a professional, and as such he had to have inner control. He knew he could play the role. He had done it so many times before.

Right behind Robin came another patrol car, his cover, driven by Harold Walles. He had been on the force about the same length of time as Robin, but was a few years younger and had come from a different background and for different reasons. Harold had a college degree in history, and had chosen police work over graduate school. He had wanted to gain some worldly experience. He also was much more attune to the idea of police work as primarily being public service, and saw real opportunity to be of value here. He understood that a police officer in his patrol car represents considerable power in the

manner in which he exercises his judgement. He can arrest or
not arrest, for example, in many borderline situations. Harold's
interest in arresting people was considerably less than Robin's.
He was more concerned with how he could help prevent crime
by generally improving the climate of society.

Through the years, though, much of his early idealism had
been dissipated. So many of the people he came into contact
with totally revolted him. They often seemed to be just one
small step from animals. More and more he came to rely
primarily on his fellow officers and their appraisal of things.
Locker room humor relieved much of his tensions. A favorite
statement of his was that a certain person's dilemma might best
be handled by "retroactive birth control." Often he resorted to
this phrase in his frustration over midnight family fights,
abused and neglected children, drunken drivers, and sexual
deviates.

He struggled to maintain his perspective, as he often
suspected that the world could not possibly be as bad as he was
beginning to see it. He often felt as if he were dealing with
problems far beyond his competence to handle. He wanted more
help, more training, but it simply was not available. He had
begun to take some college courses in psychology and sociology
during his off hours, but these were of questionable value. He
often found himself silently downgrading his teachers and his
fellow students. They seemed to live in an unreal world, to be
quite naive. Only he and his fellow officers really knew what life
was all about.

Despite their differences he felt a special kinship to Robin
Wells. This feeling heightened as he drew his car up behind
Robin's. They were two comrades going into battle together.
The rest of the world was happily oblivious to this little drama
before them. The doctors and the social workers were enjoying
their backyard barbecues. Society labeled these poeple as
helpers, but where was their help now? And what about the
judges? Tonight he and Robin would risk their lives trying to
"cool off these two screaming idiots." And, if an arrest should be
made, next week the judge would give out some sort of
suspended sentence. That is, if the district attorney would even
be willing to prosecute.

The only one that Harold could rely on at this moment was
Robin. And Robin could rely only on Harold. They glanced at

one another and their eyes met as they got out of their cars and began to enter the fray. Another crisis for these comrades in arms to handle. And yet, after all the tension and shouting was over, who would thank or commend them? Not even their fellow officers. For, after all, what is "the big deal about breaking up two nuts fighting on a street?"

The story will be stopped at this point. Let us assume that the two officers acted efficiently and succeeded in settling the crisis. They first separated the disputants, Robin talking with Stephen and Harold talking with the neighbor. They listened to the two separate complaints for awhile, attempting to calm the two combatants. When tempers had settled the two officers held a brief conference and returned to the other two men. Robin told Stephen that it was a public street and that he had no legal right to object. But he did sympathize with him, and said that his partner would ask the neighbor to perhaps park elsewhere, just to help keep the peace. Then Robin made a bit of a threat, stating that such arguing in the street could lead to a disturbing the peace charge. Meanwhile, Harold made that same threat to the neighbor, agreed that he did have the legal right to park anywhere on the street, but advised him to park elsewhere to keep the peace. Things were settled down for the night at least when the officers left.

The events in the preceeding story will be used to illustrate topics to be discussed in the succeeding chapters. Such calls are not at all rare for police. Calls of this sort, only vaguely involving criminal activity, actually make up the bulk of police calls. Police do much social work. This point will be made in the chapter dealing with the police caseload.

Regarding the conflict between Stephen Stone and his neighbor, how capable are the two officers of diagnosing the core of the problem as being Stephen's paranoid thinking? Have they been trained to recognize a paranoid, and do they have some guidelines for dealing with one? Do they know about the so-called *critical distance*, the physical and psychological safe space between him and others that the paranoid needs? Do they fully understand the necessity for clear, concrete, firm and consistent communication when dealing with a paranoid? And most important of all, do they have a grasp of the tremendous rage in a paranoid and how he provokes this same rage in others, making the temptation to retaliate in kind the main obstacle in working with such a person?

Is there really any help for a man like Stephen Stone, or is he doomed to a life of angry mistrust and trouble making? Does the average community have services available to him? Would he use those services?

Is society demanding too much of the police in asking them to approach such complicated interpersonal problems? Perhaps some other sort of person should be responsible for a call such as this.

Does the cooling off of the immediate crisis in any way approach the basic problems? What about the Stone children, watching from the home as the drama in the street progresses? Should anyone be concerned about the impact of all this on them? What attitudes are they forming about the police and the world at large? Will they have problems similar to their father's some day?

Will these officers hear more about Stephen Stone? Do they have available to them a consultant, other than their sergeant, who can help them understand what is going on? Would some sort of follow-up be indicated here, before the next crisis erupts?

These are just a few of the questions that a call like this provokes. They are questions that will be asked repeatedly throughout this book. There are no definitive answers to these questions, but there are some approximate answers, or approaches, which will be discussed.

One approach, of course, is better police training with more emphasis on the science of human behavior. Perhaps all policemen should be expected to be mental health paraprofessionals, just like the army corpsman who works in a mental hygiene clinic as a psychiatrist's assistant. Or perhaps each department should have some policemen designated as specialists in this area, and they should respond to certain types of calls. Chapter III will include some experiences in training police in human behavior.

Another approach would be to have trained mental health professionals work more closely with the police. A predominant theme of this book, drawn from experience, is that in many ways police and the caseload they treat have been deserted by the mental health profession. Some actual case examples can best illustrate this point.

A police officer was called to intervene in a rather bloody fist fight between a father and his seventeen-year-old son. The officer broke up the fight and interviewed the participants and other family members. He found that the son's behavior had become increasingly strange in recent months. The son had become withdrawn and seemed preoccupied with the idea that his father was plotting to kill him. The son had rather unexpectedly attacked the father, who defended himself, and the police had been called.

The officer was impressed with a certain strangeness in the son, and he became convinced that the boy was mentally ill. He took the son to the emergency room of the county hospital where a doctor agreed to hold the boy overnight for the probate court, stating that he thought him to be schizophrenic. The son was committed to a state hospital the next day.

Three weeks later the officer called the state hospital and talked to the social worker assigned to the case. The officer explained who he was and asked how the boy was doing and when he might be released. The social worker rather curtly told the officer that information of that sort was rather privileged and available only to mental health people involved in the case. The officer slammed the phone down in a huff.

* * * *

A police officer found a young man in his early twenties wandering aimlessly through the park. As the officer watched, the man almost walked in front of a car. The officer approached the man and was greeted with a rather blank stare. Then the man finally spoke, but he was rather disorganized and hard to follow. The officer put the man in his car and took him to the emergency room of the local county hospital. There a resident psychiatrist examined the man and told the officer that he suspected chronic schizophrenia. The officer asked the resident to admit the man, but the resident refused. He did not think the man was an immediate danger to himself or others. He told the officer that he would make an appointment for the man in the outpatient clinic for the following morning. He would also give the man a few tranquillizers to take until then.

"But what do I do with him tonight?" the officer asked.

"That's your problem," the resident replied. "This is a hospital, not a boarding home."

So the officer took the man back to the park, turned him loose and hurried away, trying hard to control his rage.

* * * *

Of course this problem is not all the fault of mental health people, as the following example shows.

A juvenile court counselor was working with an angry young man who always talked about his hatred for police. He began more and more to talk about killing some "pigs." He said he had some weapons hidden away, and he spoke of killing himself in a shootout with "the pigs." This would be a good way to go, he reasoned, since he would take some police along with him.

The counselor became more and more apprehensive and decided that he should share some information with the police. By phone he contacted the police captain in charge of the area where the young man resided. The counselor briefly told the captain the situation and stated that he would like to have a meeting with the patrolman assigned to the boy's neighborhood. By working together, perhaps they could prevent a disaster.

The captain said he and his men did not have time for such things. He politely thanked the counselor and hung up.

In any event, there certainly is a gap between the police officer and the mental health professional, even though they both deal with the same problems and have the same goals of a more safe, sane and sensible society. In Chapters IV and V of this book, attempts to bridge this gap by having social workers labor along-side the police are discussed.

In Chapter VI, human behavior specialists will direct to police some observations gleaned from working with them. Members of the mental health professions are coming to respect police more and more and to have considerable compassion for them, as they are often caught in the middle of a rapidly changing culture. Thus, the authors consider themselves friends of the police. But, like most of us, police do bring some of their problems on themselves.

Chapter VII will be addressed to nonpolice, especially the

authors' colleagues in those fields that are more commonly accepted as being strictly social service. In some ways they will be mildly chastised for attitudes of isolation from and denial of a whole problem population that often the police alone are forced to deal with.

The last chapter of this book will give some impressions and concerns for society, a society where the pendulum is swinging more and more toward individual freedom and away from deference to authority such as that of the policeman. The authors believe in authority and do not think that society can survive without it. The individual is challenged to maturely recognize this, and authority is challenged to become more worthy of its power. Ideas about a more ideal police system for the future are presented.

It is our hope that this little book might be of some value to teachers in police science, social work and related disciplines. With that in mind, each chapter will be followed by some questions for discussion which focus on the main points we have tried to make in the chapter.

As a closure to this introductory chapter, the authors feel that a more complete explanation of who *we* are is in order. One author is a psychiatrist, and the other is a psychiatric social worker with an additional degree in public health. We began our work with police in the fall of 1970, about four and one half years ago, as staff members of what is now known as the Multnomah County (Oregon) Law Enforcement Counseling Program (MCLECP). Initially the program was known as the Family Crisis Project of the Columbia Region Association of Governments. The program is a modest one. Currently it consists of one full-time psychiatric social worker, a part-time psychiatrist and a part-time secretary. A few students, usually from the fields of social work, general medicine and psychiatry, regularly bolster the manpower.

The original goal of the program was to somehow aid the police in one particularly troublesome and dangerous call, the family fight. This goal soon broadened, however, to help police officers in all of the varied noncriminal, social service aspects of their jobs. Initiated with federal funds from the Law Enforcement Assistance Administration but now supported totally with local money, this program has worked mainly within the Multnomah County Sheriff's Department. This department consists of 250 sworn personnel serving a combined rural and urban population of about 167,000. The city of Portland is within Multnomah County but is a separate jurisdiction. The department has a history of progressiveness and has received national recognition for being the first nonfederal law enforcement agency to require a baccalaureate degree for new officers.

Initially, the MCLECP had primarily a training function. It offered practical training in human behavior to officers in a variety of settings. A unique aspect of the training was supervised police interaction with people in emotional crisis. For example, as part of a week-long course entitled "Understanding People," police actually did the intake work at a local mental health clinic.

Training, however, soon became a relatively secondary function. The MCLECP staff realized that there were few social services available after normal business hours. Often in the middle of the night and pressured by time constraints, the police officer was on his own in trying to solve complicated "people problems."

In the fall of 1971, attempting to respond to the need, the MCLECP staff undertook a rather uncertain venture. They contacted students from the Graduate School of Social Work at Portland State University, who usually obtained their field experience through assignment to a traditional mental health agency, such as an out-patient clinic. As a result, three students were assigned for their field placements to the Operations Division Headquarters of the Sheriff's department.

The expectation was that the patrol car would serve as clinic or office. The MCLECP staff was responsible for supervising the clinical aspects of the students' work, while the commander of the swing shift was responsible for their administrative supervision. Each student was paired with a volunteer uniformed officer, and one night a week they operated as a "counseling team" from a patrol car. A team was thus available three nights of the week. The dispatcher sent them to those calls which seemed appropriate, such as family fights, attempted suicides, neighborhood disputes, etc. The goals were to expand police service and to free the district officer from such calls. It was also hoped that the experiment would make the social service community more aware of the type of work police were often called upon to do.

The experiment was a modest success, and as a result, the MCLECP decided to expand the social work aspect of the program. A full-time psychiatric social worker was added to the staff. His job was loosely defined as a "police social worker," working in the field after hours in support of the police. He remained in this role for twenty months until a severe local budget crunch temporarily eliminated the position. Still, much was learned from the experience.

With some modifications the small MCLECP staff is still involved in training police and in giving them direct support in the field. We do not claim tremendous success for our program, however. The program has survived to some degree in a time of local financial crisis, and outside evaluations have been quite complimentary. But often its acceptance, both by the police system and the mental health system, has left a good deal to be desired. While no one has really obstructed us to any great extent, neither have we received a great deal of encouragement from important police personnel. Generally, the patrolman on the street has accepted us much more readily than the administration.

Most discouraging is the fact that there has not been the expansion of the program that we constantly hope for. But we persevere, talking to people, writing articles and now even a book, because we think the ideas we are developing make a lot of sense.

Questions for Discussion:

1. What do the authors mean by police social work?
2. In your experience do police do much of what might be termed social work?
3. Are you aware of bad feelings between police and others whose job it is to help people?
4. What might be done to increase communication and understanding between police and other helping groups such as social workers, psychiatrists, ministers and the like?
5. What is a paranoid, and how frequently do you think paranoid thinking is responsible for human problems?

6. Can you give some examples of times when you exhibit paranoid thinking by projecting your own feelings on to someone else?

Chapter II

THE POLICE CASELOAD*

HELP is not just another of those dirty little four letter words. Police service, or the helping of others, is a vital part of the police function. It is also one of the ways your community gets to know and trust the police. It has always been so: The police system is measured by the community as much by the skills of its police service encounters as by the smartness of its hardware or by the latest published crime statistics. *The police officer, and eventually the police system, succeeds or fails on the quality of the individual officer as a concerned human being.*

In recent years there has been a growing recognition among police officers that service is an accepted part of their work, and that it should be supported by training. The double advantages of a skilled approach are in more effective help to the citizen in crisis and in greater safety for the officer. As with every other skill, some officers are by nature more adept in human encounters than others, but all can learn.

The term *police caseload* refers to those who are the recipients of police service. In this chapter something of the variety and complexity of the police caseload will be discussed with the aid of true case examples. Service can be an important element of any police call. Some calls, however, demand much more of the officer in service capability. The cases that will be presented here are very strongly service calls, and for that reason have been termed the *police caseload.* The cases presented were handled very well. Comments on the cases presented here are only for clarification or further expansion on some particular point.[1]

---

*In this chapter the authors have tried, through the presentation of case examples, to illustrate some of the convictions developed over these past four years of involvement with police officers.

[1]Lauer has further researched the police caseload. Colbach, E., Fosterling, C., and Lauer, R.: Police *are* mental caregivers. *Police Chief,* 40:49-51, November, 1973.

MRS. SOAMES AND DYNAMITE

This call occurred early in one social worker's contact with
the police system. If he were, as it had been decided, to play a
part in police training, he should see what an officer does. So on
a clear, warm evening in August he found himself riding on
patrol with an officer we shall call Dan Brogan. Dan, a first-
name kind of man, was a veteran of some twelve years of police
work. He was relaxed, confident, and a comfortable person to be
with. The radio kept them continually informed that crises were
occurring about the city, but outside their district. As the
evening wore on, both grew more hopeful of some kind of
action and excitement.

They finally got their call, a possible prowler, and an address.
Officer Brogan wrote it down, laughed and said, "Well, at least
this will give you a chance to meet Mrs. Soames."

He turned the car and drove some distance into one of the
older sections of the city, still residential but with unpainted
houses, unkept lawns and poorly maintained roads. The
address was that of a small, drab house. The wooden porch
slanted, and it had obviously been many years since repairs of
any kind had been done.

Mrs. Soames, to whom Dan introduced the social worker, was
a tiny, talkative lady in her seventies. She assured them that
there had been noises in the back yard, and she thought that
someone might have crawled in the basement window. Officer
Brogan said he would look around. They had been standing in
what might be described as an old parlor, a room crowded with
furniture looking both uncomfortable and unused. Dan
obviously knew the house, since he moved off through an
adjoining room into the kitchen, and could be heard going
down a flight of stairs. Mrs. Soames invited the young social
worker into the other room and settled herself into an old
platform rocker. At her request he sat down on a nearby dining
room chair. She then began to "visit," with apparently no
further concern about prowlers. She did not seem too surprised
when Officer Brogan returned to report no signs of entry. As
they were about to leave, Mrs. Soames did ask if one of them
might tie another string to her kitchen light, as the string had
broken earlier that evening. She had string, so they tied it for

her. She returned the remainder of her tangled string collection back to her cupboard drawer, thanked them and opened the door for them to leave.

Officer Brogan said he did not particularly mind this kind of call. Such calls might bend the rules a little, but they certainly did not hurt anyone. Mrs. Soames was alone, with no family in town. He reasoned that she occasionally got a little lonely or afraid and needed some human contact. It was a fairly simple matter, and as he said, he had a grandmother himself.

Mrs. Soames was part of what Officer Brogan called "my caseload." Dan's "caseload" covered those people of his district whom he saw for varied problems which were only partially law enforcement.

To dispel the thought that all such calls were easy, he then described one that occurred in another police department where he had worked. He and a partner had gone on a domestic disturbance call and found themselves suddenly facing a shotgun. It had taken both a great deal of talking and careful maneuvering to get out of that one. The thing he remembered most was the tense explosiveness of this man with the gun, who was furious beyond reason. The key issue had revolved around a policeman who will be called Johnson, who was hated by the man. Dan had never met Officer Johnson but did know of him by reputation. Johnson was an officer who defined himself as "a tough cop," and one who was often known to "put people down." Dan said that call had been the lesson of a lifetime for him. Johnson had been able to make at least one enemy for life, and the life had almost turned out to be Dan's. He was never too sure just what Johnson had done, but he was sure that this man with the gun was dynamite, and Johnson, Dan believed, had somehow lit a slow fuse.

Dan Brogan had thought about this a good deal since. He decided that he did not just represent himself out there on a call, but every officer who might someday have to deal with the involved citizen. "I have one basic rule," he said, "I never take away a man's self-respect."

That evening, early in his contact with the police system, the social worker was presented with the extremes of the police caseload. Police service calls range from the dull to the dangerous.

Within this range of calls are all the human pressures of living that can at times push any of us beyond rational control. Police service is a part of such calls labelled as abuse, neglect, exposure, suicide, accidental death, runaway, incest, parent-child conflict, domestic disturbance, unwanted, psychotic, or any of a number of other dispatch labels.

The lessons of Dan's cases are important ones. No officer can afford to handle a call badly or even indifferently. The reputations, if not the lives of other police officers are at stake. In this sense there is no routine or "chippy" call. *A police officer's contact is always significant to the citizen.*

PETER

Peter was working again. It was good to have money. He had borrowed a lot recently and might or might not pay some of it back. It depended mostly on how much he was pushed by any of the lenders. A couple of the women, he knew, would never get their money. In fact, he would probably work them for even more later. They were the "victim" types, there to be taken. To his mind, "they just asked for it."

Others he would stall if he could, or pay if he must, and if he happened to have the money. Of course, he could always just pick up and go.

Pete was one of those people who moved if the pressure got too great. A boss hustling him to work, the police "on his tail" over someone's missing property, or maybe some friends wanting more than he was ready to give — keep moving and you never get nailed.

Pete did not mind people, but he wanted them on *his* terms and not too close either. There were just two types of people in his world: those who "screwed" and those who got "screwed." He knew which one he planned to be.

It was Saturday afternoon, and his "wife," the woman he was now living with, was out shopping. Her two young boys were around the neighborhood somewhere. June, his legal wife, had packed her bags a month ago and moved out. She accused him of beating her. He had on occasion, but she had deserved it. If she did not want to get hit, she should have kept her mouth shut.

Grace had moved in shortly after this anyway, so he had not really lost anything. If he someday got divorced and married Grace, she would be this third legal wife. But he doubted that they would ever get that far.

He watched football for awhile and then got bored. After two more beers he switched off the television and wandered through the house. It was junky. Grace ought to get her tail moving and clean it up.

He had money — what the hell. He would go down to Smitty's and see what was happening there. The car had plenty of gas. Smitty's would have broads on the bar stools, shuffleboard and some action. There had been one hell of a fight down there last week.

Pete got home at eleven. It had been good, but he still would have liked something more to happen. The evening really did not seem finished yet. His mother had always said that Pete was a doer, not a thinker. Something needed to be done.

Grace was still up. She was out on the couch, in her nightgown, watching some T.V. talk show. Nothing duller. The place looked even junkier than it had this afternoon. Pete suddenly felt mad, damned mad. Grace was not going to get by with this. Action was coming, and he felt exhilarated.

It was almost twelve when he heard someone knocking at the door. He knew right away who it would be. Some snoopy son-of-a-bitching neighbor had called the cops again. Why wouldn't people just leave him alone? If he and Grace wanted to fight, that was their business.

Pete and Grace are certainly part of the police caseload. So are her two boys. Officers wish they would seek their help elsewhere, but they never will. Pete and Grace live in the present, the immediate present. Their problem was Saturday night. Monday morning was a world away. They would never arrive at the agencies to which they might be referred. And if they did, what could they say of their problems? Pete's "not a talker, he's a doer." Besides that, he does not have a problem anyway. "If Grace and the others would just do what they were supposed to, there would be no trouble," he would say.

"The fight all had to do with the beer. A guy has a few drinks and things may hit him just a little wrong. You know how it is.

"Who can talk to a social worker anyway? They keep asking

how you feel about something. Who the hell ever knows how they feel? You just do. They keep wanting to make appointments. Having you come in at some regular time each week and sit down in some little office and talk. It's all a bunch of crap."

As the reader may by now suspect, Pete and Grace are at the heart of the police caseload. What help they are to receive, and this may be minimal, will come about only through the intervention of authority.

The authors would say that Pete and Grace are examples of a character disordered population. Their ways are learned early, well set and a part of their total life patterns. The patterns of this case example show impulsiveness and explosiveness. One would expect such a family to present difficulties for society in many of the ways they interface with others. Police officers particularly could expect to come into contact with them. The call might well range from a driving violation through those related to alcohol, sexual misconduct or even extreme violence.

They form a significant and worrisome part of any police caseload. Unfortunately, such people are very difficult to change by any of the talking therapies alone. It is possible that change might be effected through a judicious use of both authority and directive counseling provided at those times of necessary intervention. If their problem is "experienced" at 11:00 P.M. Saturday night, any resolution of it must certainly be "experienced" then too.

* * * *

BILLY BOY

Joan, Sergeant Baker of the Sheriff's Juvenile Division, sat in the living room talking with Billy and his parents. Billy was a runaway. He was now back home after his latest disappearance, having been "turned in" by a store manager across town. To Joan it seemed there were elements of planning in this, as if the manager, almost in spite of himself, had been somehow made aware of Billy. In fact, there was a great deal of the staged quality of Billy's explanation of how he had come to run and in what had subsequently happened to him. Joan mentally tried to sort out the causes into "good reasons" and "real reasons."

The good reasons, as explained by Billy, had to do with his father's anger about his poor report card. He knew as well that his father expected more of him in school and would be disappointed too. Billy was bright and could have done well but usually did not. Would he have been badly punished? From what Joan knew of them, he would not have been. Did Billy really believe it would have been so bad? When pushed he had to admit that no such mistreatment had occurred in the past.

Yet Billy needed a reason to run. His mother, in looking back, could now describe ways in which he had prepared for each running. She always had noted a certain anxiety and nervousness on his part before, contrasted to the relaxed and satisfied look upon each return. It was as if he had gone out to prove something and had done so. What had he proven?

The case was technically over. It could be closed now that Billy was back home again. Sergeant Baker decided not to close this one, however, at least not for herself. In her six years at Sheriff's Juvenile, she had begun to notice a pattern in the records of children seen for serious crimes and repeating problems. Almost all had their first notation in the record as a *runaway*. Many times the report was made by telephone, and the case was closed by phone as well when the child returned. He or she was never seen nor the reasons for running discussed. Perhaps it was time the police department, a social agency, or someone took a more serious look at the runaway. Maybe this is the only way some kids can say, "I'm facing more than I can handle right now."

Sergeant Baker was able to fit two more visits with Billy into her already tight schedule. From talks with both Billy and his parents, she pieced together the following story.

Billy was not really their son but was part of the family. The mother's niece, a "wild" girl and most indifferent mother, had borne Billy between marriages.

He had been "fathered" by one of a number of casual boyfriends. The girl never wanted him. She had kept him off and on for his first three years, twice leaving him with them and then appearing to take him away again. On both occasions he had been left with them, Billy had shown many signs of his mother's indifferent care and overt anger. There had been open sores, scars and obvious malnutrition. The last time they had told her she could only leave him if it was to be on a permanent basis. They would adopt him, which they did.

In his talks with Joan, Billy's stories were marked with one main theme: his ability to take care of himself. Each runaway established for him that he could survive separate and independent of anyone's love. His favorite story was of a blackberry patch. In the midst of those brambles, down a narrow overgrown path just big enough for him to crawl through, was a small clearing. In this clearing someone had left an old sheet of corregated iron, a few boards and a tattered quilt. With some quart bottles filled with water, he could have lived there. He assured Joan that he could have eaten the berries, been protected by the brambles and slept rolled in the quilt, safe from the rain under the sheet of corregated iron.

The preceeding story should give the reader a good idea as to why Billy runs. His life was programmed early, and he has something to prove. He learned before he even had words for it that in being dependent one tends to become vulnerable, and to be vulnerable was to risk death. Whenever Billy finds himself beginning to need others, a warning is sounded, and he must move away.

Others will run away for other reasons, such as panic at the sexual demands of incest, the frustration of coping with a psychotic parent or perhaps a growing awareness that they can never satisfy the demands of a parent to be the best athlete or an *A* student. Knowing *why*, however, may give the involved social worker a grasp of the problem.

Billy's future is not hard to predict. Without major psychological treatment he will continue into what the authors term a sociopathic (or psychopathic or antisocial) personality. Whatever the term used, this group reproduces itself generation by generation, and Billy's children may turn out not too dissimilar from their grandmother before them.

Perhaps this is the proper time to discuss sociopaths. Police officers will see far more than their share of such individuals. Where do they come from? They are the product of their environment. The sociopath has in almost every known instance experienced early emotional or physical neglect or abuse. The sociopath is one extreme form of that larger category, the "character disorder," which has been discussed previously.

As did Billy, sociopaths learn early never to trust or place emotional investment in other human beings. People are objects to be used. In manipulating them they can reassert their own power and again feel secure. They hurt many people around them in this way, particularly those closest and most involved.

Police officers are "taken in" by sociopaths many times, since in their professional duties they come in contact with so many of them. There are two good procedures for quick analyzation of the sociopathic character. The first is to ask oneself, "Is this person too good to be true?" Somewhere inside oneself a warning bell should go off anytime a person seems to be pleasing almost beyond belief.

The ultimate test, of course, is in whether what they do or have done corresponds to what they say. What is the "track record?" Chamelion-like, sociopaths are extremely adept at matching their color to their immediate environment. Their immediate environment may well be a police officer and how to "please" him. Short background questioning will usually show signs of shallow emotional roots, broken marriages, abandoned children, the changing of jobs, friends or cities.

No one is going to change the sociopath to any great extent. Some sociopaths are said to just "burn out." Perhaps they just become more adept at self-management as they grow older. There is no one who really knows. Their trouble to others generally brings some for themselves as well. "Burning out" may be partially the learning process of how to avoid the inconvenience of such trouble.

Police officers can certainly help in this process. The most important step in helping the sociopath is in not being seduced and manipulated. They need to be handled "by the book." This is not only for society's best interest but for their own as well.

One of the most important services society can perform is a preventive one. This is in moving in quickly whenever signs of serious neglect or abuse are noted. This is crime prevention if anything is. Billy could have been saved if spotted earlier. There is little question but that his record will move on from the juvenile into the adult file. Often authorities seem to bend over backward to keep children with their natural parents, even when their natural parents give many clues that they do not want them and are destroying them.

TIMMY

Timmy was a stocky, alert, bright boy of nine. He was attentive and questioning, and his eyes noted everything as he rode along in the back of the police car. He was on his way to the receiving home where he would be temporarily housed until foster care plans could be made with welfare. There was an appealing quality about Timmy that the officer initially found himself responding to. Before the ride was over, however, he felt himself drawing away from the boy. The boy's questions and demands continued with no letup or apparent satisfaction. "What would the home be like? Who would they meet? What other children would be there? Where would his bed be? How long would he stay there?" Question led to question, but none to the answers Timmy seemed to need.

Then it hit him. This boy did not relate to people but to things. Schedules, buildings, objects were things he could trust, but people he could *not* trust. The officer's warmth, interest and concern were not going to reach this kid.

The trip over, the officer and Timmy walked up the steps to the home where they met the director, Mr. Morrison. As the officer introduced the two, Mr. Morrison smiled and said, "Timmy, I'm glad to meet you."

Timmy lurched back two steps and asked in a frightened voice, "Pleased to *beat* me?"

The misinterpretation of the director's greeting says a lot about Timmy's view of the world.

Timmy is trouble on the way. He has developed little control over his emotions. He is easily threatened, seeing the world as a dangerous place and expecting attack by others, and aggressively ready to defend himself. This is not the last time a police officer will be involved in Timmy's life.

What do child therapists and those who have to think in terms of helping a boy like Timmy have to take into consideration? The

important factors are pretty much the same as for helping anyone:
1. What is the degree of damage? How much has it become a part of the person, as shown in his overall pattern of relating to others?
2. How long has it been going on?

Timmy in nine years had experienced more loss, fear, pain and frustration than most of us do in a lifetime: illigitimate, abandoned, neglected and finally intentionally physically abused. But Timmy survived, and he also learned. If one had watched Timmy in action, one would have seen him guided by fairly simple but rigid rules. These rules had been learned so early in life that they seemed never to have reached his head but remained at gut level and basic to all life encounters. Put into words they would have been:
1. Others cannot be trusted, so one can only depend on oneself.
2. People will hurt you if they can.
3. The world is a dangerous place.
4. The most feared thing is love, since it makes one vulnerable.

How long has Timmy's problem existed? Only nine years, but in Timmy's case this is all of his life. One must also point out this damage occurred during those early years when basic relationship patterns are established. For those reasons officers are urged to be particularly aware of the children they come across in their work.

The second theme that Timmy illustrates is that of expectation or projection. This is more commonly spoken of as "the self-fulfilling prophesy." Timmy has been well conditioned by life. He *knows* what to expect and will probably be vaguely uncomfortable whenever things do not occur as they "should." It is really beside the point that much of the "should" is negative.

Is there a more direct lesson in this case for officers and their expectations of others? The authors think so.

A police officer experiences many negatives in his day-to-day working life. It must be hoped that he also does not hear "pleased to beat me" in those situations when "pleased to meet you" was really intended.

It can happen for officers, as it did for Timmy, that abuse becomes the expectation. Expectations seek fulfillment. Once established, this is a most difficult cycle to break.

CHRISTMAS EVE

It was a cold and blustery Christmas Eve, with a few inches of snow on the ground and more expected before morning. It was 9:26 P.M. when Officer Wilson was given the call "unwanted" man and an apartment address. Having been told this was probably a good "family beef" evening, a social worker was riding along. Wilson was young and had recently completed his human relations training, and the social worker was interested in seeing how he would handle such a call.

The area they entered was a "strip highway" of mixed stores, small business, drive-ins, houses and apartment complexes. The address was at one of the latter. Back past a series of apartment buildings with parking areas for each, they found their address. Two reserve officers pulled up at the same time, and Wilson and the social worker went on up to the door.

They were met by a small, attractive blond woman around age forty. Her only comment was, "Just get him out of here," spoken in a tone somewhere between anger and hysteria. They entered a living room which was warm, clean and furnished in what one might call "Montgomery Ward modern." All the appropriate items were there, including coffee table, couches, end tables, lamps, and pictures. There was nothing personal, however, except for the two motorcycle magazines and a packet of cigarettes and matches on one table.

In the corner made by the two joining couches was the visiting "boy friend." In front of him was a long, low coffee table with the lone Christmas decoration, a heavy glass candlestick holding a long white candle. As they came in he reached over, grabbed the candlestick, and said, "You sons of bitches aren't taking me out of here." He was clearly drunk and angry and possibly dangerous. He was, however, willing to talk. Wilson was also, so they sat down to hear him out.

John was twenty-nine years old and had been involved with Mary for about a year and a half. In fact, they had previously been living together in another apartment of this same building until four months ago. At that time she had also "called the cops" to have him thrown out. He pointed out there were not enough police officers to do the job now. It had taken five officers that time. When they met the apartment house manager later in the parking lot, he substantiated this, and added that they had taken out a door and window as well. Wilson assured John that he could be taken, it was just a matter of numbers, but that he would rather handle this differently if that were possible. Wilson was calm, quiet spoken, reasonable, and willing to listen. He was, at the same time, in no way intimidated or controlled by John's threats.

Wilson really listened, which people seldom do. He did not interrupt with advice or argue with John as to whether he was interpreting his experiences correctly. He did not tell John what he should have done nor did he mouth the false assurances that so many do when told of another's problems and frustrations.

Wilson tried to do just one thing, to understand. To understand quickly and simply where John was coming from, why he was angry and where the central issues lay. He did the same with Mary. It is always interesting to observe how little talking a good interviewer does.

As the officer and social worker listened, it became clear that a number of things were accomplished for both Mary and John in this "calling the cops" routine. The ones probably least in control and most used by this were the police officers themselves.

Police officers, of course, are obliged to come when a citizen is in danger. It can be concluded, however, that Mary derived some clear rewards from such danger. There was the satisfaction of provoking these situations and at the same time avoiding the results of John's anger and frustration. The officers could be used as her "champions" and were thus an extension of her power over John. The intensity of John's feelings for her were demonstrated in his forcible arrest and said much to her of her value and desirability as a woman.

John, for his part, could maintain his relationship with Mary by continuing to meet her needs in this manner. He demonstrated his manliness in such an arrest and could release some of his pent up frustration with Mary into the physical confrontation with the police officer.

None of us would define this as a healthy or mature relationship. It was also not a totally satisfactory one for either Mary or John. Through a short period of listening, the social worker helped both John and Mary to avoid one more repetition of this destructive pattern.

Once heard, John was quite willing to bargain if she would just talk privately with him for five minutes. Mary accepted, as perhaps this appeared simplest for her too.

The officer and the social worker were not made aware of the entire conversation in the kitchen. They did remain nearby in case things got out of hand again. Things did not, and John came back into the living room ready to leave, abiding by his agreement. A friend of John's (one who was still sober) had been called, and he came over to drive him away. John insisted on shaking hands all around with Officer Wilson and the social worker.

Wilson could not say whether it was Christmas Eve or just his laziness that led him to manage this call as he had. He did point out that the entire call had taken thirty minutes, while arresting John, transporting him and writing it up would have taken three times that. He then radioed in, noting "situation handled," and they moved back on patrol.

The social worker was impressed. A feeling of good will toward the police had been established. This is surely worth achieving on Christmas Eve and at other times as well. Although nothing earthshaking had occurred, both John and Mary were satisfied by the outcome. No one got "bent or bruised." What more could one ask?

They had barely gotten themselves settled into patrolling when they heard that an officer in a nearby district had caught a burglar. Wilson lit up with excitement and turned to the social worker saying, "Now that's *real* police work."

Why do Wilson and other officers as well define part of their job as "real police work" and the other as not? Officer Wilson's feelings about this are not unique. Many officers downgrade service far more than he. Many of those unfortunately do not have his natural ability to move smoothly through the anger and frustration of another's personal problems.

As you may note, the system itself does not acknowledge or credit much of the good work that is done in police service. Wilson's handling of this problem is officially recorded only in terms of his "coding off," providing for the dispatcher a combination of letter and number indicating that the call was handled. It indicates for file purposes that he coped but tells nothing of the nature of the difficulty or of his techniques and procedures for handling it. Little recognition is accorded such work either by police departments or fellow officers.

For the most part the police system, Wilson, his fellow officers and recruits still learn to handle such cases through "war stories," the brief observations of other officers in action, or through trial and error. These situations are too sensitive and potentially dangerous to be left to such continued casual learning.

THE GOOD CASE

It was an extremely cold and rainy Saturday night. A social worker and an officer were at a hospital emergency room. The officer was inside getting information from the accident victim, a young man we will call Bill, who was frightened and still in pain. He had miscalculated both his own skill and the maneuverability of his motorcycle. The bike was a mess, and a friend with a pickup truck had already taken it on home. The young man was indeed very lucky to be alive and under medical care.

Three of Bill's friends sat on a bench in the waiting room, planning to see him when the doctors finished. They were quiet but whispered occasionally to each other. The words were not distinguishable, but the tones were those of suspicion and resentment. In the brief exchange the social worker had with one of them he was clearly told that they had little respect for any of the "establishment," including the hospital they were then in.

He left them "pleasuring" in their resentment at the world and went over to talk with the ambulance attendant. The attendant was young and efficient. The social worker had seen him in action on other occasions in the past. He took his work seriously and enjoyed telling about it.

As he talked about this case, one could see that he took great pride in his work. He described the quick judgements required and the importance of good, fast emergency care on the site of an accident. "It's often determined then whether a person really lives or dies. If we don't make it, the hospital can't."

In talking about his job, the young ambulance attendant went on to tell about "good cases." These were not simple cases, pleasant cases or even necessarily successful ones. A "good case," it developed, was one in which he could use his skill, and put into practice the training he had received, testing his abilities against all those possibilities of death.

The social worker could not help but relate the "good case" to an often heard remark from officers with whom he traveled about "real police work." It reminded him also that every profession has its "good cases." If you were to ask, for example, any of the mental health professionals you would probably learn that "acting-out" disorders were not "good cases," while verbal, insightful, well-motivated, neurotic people were.

There are a number of points to be considered from this case example. One of the most significant is the pleasure everyone takes in a job well done. The ambulance attendant knew his job and could, therefore, measure his own performance.

What if he had been trained for one task but sent out to do another? It is suspected that he would have become both confused and angry. Here again, the issue of "police service" becomes important.

The authors believe that "police service" is a task worthy of pride. Done well it contributes to a better community, and most probably to a more peaceful one. If, as police officers insist, it is most of what they do, it should receive training, time, recognition and acceptance.

To date many officers define service as a burden to police work rather than an opportunity. It detracts from their time on patrol, isolated from the public but attached by the electronic umbilical cord to the precinct and all other cars on patrol. The authors suggest that officers would be relieved of a psychological bind in the recognition by the police system itself of the importance of the service it provides. The officer would then be doing "legitimate" police work in a much larger proportion of his assigned calls.

To the degree that the officer's working world is out of alignment with his expectations, he, too, is subject to cynicism and resentment. Like Bill's friends, it is far too easy for any of us to then smolder in quiet anger, shared only with other members of "the club." No one wishes to have a police system that thinks of itself only as a persecuted elite.

THE SIMPLE SOLUTION

The social worker had been asked to help out with the new recruit academy. His task was to present in a two-hour time period all the information a recruit might need on the "domestic disturbance." He had been doing this for a couple of years and knew a little of what to expect.

He, therefore, came prepared that morning with diagrams, an exercise, handout material and an experienced officer with whom to hold a teaching dialogue. He knew that discussing such issues with recruits would be a far different thing than with the experienced officer. Without experience to build upon, the recruits' main guideline was the manual. They relied on it extensively and wished for clear, straightforward procedures for each problem raised.

Officer Colby, who came with the social worker that morning, was to provide the field experience. His task was a very important and difficult one. Officer Colby was in many ways an interpreter. In this setting he could be said to interpret from both ends toward the middle, the recruits in this example representing this middle. Officer Colby interpreted from the "real world" of his day-to-day patrol experience. Officer Colby also interpreted from his earlier training in human relations and his knowledge of the skills and concepts of crisis counseling.

To both, these two hours seemed little enough time to devote to one of the most dangerous and frustrating calls an officer receives. Thirty young men sat with open notebooks waiting for clear instructions about how one handles what is often a very messy and individually complicated situation. Following the brief lecture, accompanied by diagrams and explanations, came the most important part of the lesson, the discussion period. In the give-and-take of this dialogue the messages presented would either be made clear or lost to the new officers.

If nothing else the two instructors were determined to get across some basic points of crisis resolution. The messages were essentially those of common sense, flexibility and a little compassion. After all, every one of us on occasion has gotten "out on a limb" and could have used a little help in getting off.

Before the two finished their presentation on this day,

however, they were given some unasked for and completely
voluntary help. An old sergeant, waiting his turn to talk about
"stolen goods," stepped in to tell the new men what he knew of
"family beefs." He obviously felt the whole problem was being
made far more involved then it need be. As he said, "I solved that
problem a long time ago. I just tell them 'If things don't
straighten up, I'll haul their kids off and get them put in foster
care.' I've done it a lot of times too."

The only comment can be, if you cannot help, at least do not
make things worse. Police officers are no different from others.
Everyone would like nice, neat solutions to human problems.
Unfortunately, there are none. Mental health professionals have
no solutions to relationship problems, just some better choices as
to how to approach those problems. This parallels the police
officer's knowledge that he will never have a solution to *crime*,
just more experience in working on crimes.

Pat solutions are dangerous. A major problem with an "answer" is that it may stop people from asking the further necessary
questions. The sergeant, it is feared, in achieving his "answer,"
long ago ceased to question his practice. His one-solution answer
was used to resolve all domestic disturbance problems, regardless
of complexity or variation.

The problem of a domestic disturbance call, in his mind, may
well have been in the police being called at all. If so, thereafter,
were he and other officers called less often? If domestic disturbance calls do diminish through such activity, may it perhaps
result only in an officer's involvement in a more deteriorated
situation later?

The authors are not suggesting that foster home placement or
that the removal of children is never indicated. It may well be the
necessary and only alternative in an extremely bad situation. One
must consider, however, to what degree parental fighting is just a
poor environment or a completely destructive one for the children
involved. If so, will the parents and/or the children profit from
foster care? It would be hoped that they do, but this is certainly far
from proven in many cases. No police officer should use such a
resource as a means of punishing a family. The cost to the child is
far too great.

The quick one-answer solution is a wrong one in most cases. The simple solution is often an indication that we simply do not understand how complicated things really are. From your own experience consider in how many instances someone else's quick or simple solution to one of your problems has been of help. As you think about this, consider also how few times others have really understood the total problem as you experienced it.

The best solution in most cases will be one that the parties involved can devise themselves. An outsider can help in guiding others into a recognition of the central issues and in considering alternatives. Beyond that, the authors would still recommend that everyone avoid advice and the "simple solution."

HALF MEASURES

It was 10:30 P.M. on a Friday evening in summer, and the social worker was again sharing patrol with an officer. It was Officer Ryan, a tall, black haired young man, extremely bright, sensitive and capable. The dispatcher asked Officer Ryan to meet a concerned neighbor lady at a particular address. Upon arriving they took flash lights and moved across the yard to a small one-story dwelling. Even in the half dark, they could note that the house had been amateurishly and cheaply built with used doors and small windows.

The neighbor who opened the door was in her late fifties. She told them that Mildred, the lady of the house, was on the floor, and she did not know what they could do about her. The inside of the house was drab, dirty and seemed quite confining to the two tall men. They were immediately aware of a rather sweet, sickening smell that was all but overpowering.

In the living room were the two occupants, a very old man sitting in a large and badly stained easy chair, and the other, Mildred, who was sitting in the middle of the floor. The old man, who appeared almost disinterested, did explain that Mildred, his housekeeper, had not fallen but just sat down that morning and seemed unwilling to get up.

Mildred, in some ways, matched the surroundings well. She was almost as old as the man himself, she being in her seventies and he well into his eighties. She was grossly overweight and had dirtied herself. She indeed showed no interest in getting up.

The social worker felt somewhat intimidated by the situation. Obviously this was a social problem. There should have been something he could recommend or advise, but unfortunately there was not. As was previously stated, it was 10:30 P.M. and a Friday evening. All the social agencies and most of the public resources were closed. Since Mildred was not injured, it seemed illogical to call an ambulance and send her to a hospital. Neither the neighbor, the officer, nor the social worker could think of any other logical course of action.

The problem seemed to center around the combination of senility with some alcohol abuse. The officer and the social worker eventually, and with some effort, hoisted Mildred onto a couch. They all agreed that some type of nursing home situation was probably appropriate for both Mildred and her employer. The neighbor lady agreed to look in again in the morning and to call a welfare agency on Monday.

This again is a typical example of police service. It is certainly not what an officer dreams of doing as he enters the force. It is, however, representative of many of the situations he faces. Problems arise in the community at times when no resources are available. The situations are depressing, and the help that can be given is minimal. The officer simply helps in making the best of a bad situation.

The authors are not suggesting that other resources should not be available. Obviously the community has in instances like this left the police system "out on a limb." Agencies should be on call and various emergency facilities should be open. Social problem situations are not limited to an eight-hour day, Monday through Friday.

Officer Ryan and the social worker both left this situation feeling somewhat guilty. There should have been more to do, but what? They discussed their actions and reassured each other in their inadequacy. Perhaps for their own comfort they did need to accept that society does not provide well for all of its citizens. For the present time social and emotional first aid may be all the police system can provide, and perhaps that is enough.

Until the community better understands police service, the system will not change. It is for this reason the authors seek to legitimatize police service both within the community and within

the police system itself. Until the community has some understanding of the extent and degree of the problems faced within the
police caseload, there will be no change. Until that day half measures may be all that Officer Ryan has to provide.

CRAZY MAN

The call from the dispatcher sent Officer Smith on his way to
an address for a contact on a mental case. A "back-up" or cover
car was dispatched to assist from the district next to his. The
area was middle class, with the houses well kept and attractive.
Smith timed his arrival well and just parked as Officer Jewett,
his cover man, drove up.

The man answering the door was in shirt sleeves but still had
his tie on. It was not quite 6:00 P.M. and Smith guessed he would
have just arrived home from work. The man introduced himself
as Mr. Gamble, and brought the officers into the living room to
meet his wife.

Mrs. Gamble sat on the couch looking very distracted and
quite miserable. Her hands were in constant motion, clutching
and fidgeting as if they were almost beyond her awareness or
control. The living room was clean and in order, reflecting well
the neatness of the woman's dress. The couple were probably in
their early fifties, and had the appearance of having lived the
years comfortably.

The Gambles told the officers that they had called about their
son. He was now in his room upstairs, as he had been all day.
The father had just come down from there when the officers
arrived. Their son, Elmer, was at this time huddled in the corner
behind a bureau, holding himself very rigidly and crying.
Elmer, who was now nineteen, was their youngest. Their other
two children were both married and out of the home.

Mr. Gamble suggested his son's condition might well have
something to do with drugs. Elmer was "their hippie." He had
dropped out of high school, lived with friends in town, and for a
short while had worked in a small leather craft shop. He had
always been good with his hands and had made beautiful belts
for his father and brother last Christmas. Two weeks ago he had
moved back home. He had seemed depressed, and his mother
thought he had broken up with some girl.

Smith did not particularly like this kind of call. Psychotics were always so damned unpredictable. Twice he had seen such people explode wildly when approached. On both occasions he had been surprised at their seemingly superhuman strength and agility. He wondered if somehow being crazy did not magnify their strength. He asked about possible weapons, guns, leather working knives, etc. They seemed shocked, and said Elmer was not like that. Smith was not particularly assured. He was glad it was Officer Jewett who was his partner on this. Jewett was big, calm and very dependable.

Smith had learned from his past experiences, and moved very slowly. He knew that when people become mentally disorganized they often become frightened as well. Others, even those trying to help, may then be seen by the disorganized person as threatening and ready to attack. Some of the strength Smith had noted may well come from the desperation of their defense against such perceived danger. The boy's position in the corner reinforced these thoughts in Smith's mind, and he decided not to hurry this one along.

Talking in a low and calm voice, he moved slowly forward and sat on the edge of the bed. Although Elmer gave no indication, Smith felt the boy did know they were there. Smith told him what they would be doing and repeated this slowly several times. He assured him that he had nothing to be afraid of, that they would not hurt him. Officer Smith was patient, and eventually Elmer turned his head to look at them.

This all took time, but Smith was now at a point in his career when he would much rather talk than fight. He thought it better police work as well. A short time later, with some further reassurance and encouragement from Smith, Elmer did stand up. He then seemed willing to talk a little as well, but his thoughts were not coherent or logical. He was still disorganized and scared but would go to the hospital with them.

With Elmer in the car and on their way to the hospital emergency, Smith reviewed his handling of the case. He wondered what might have happened if it had been handled by one of the less experienced, newer men who might have tended to rush things. He had been very aware as Elmer stood up that there had been a knife. It lay on the floor in the corner where he had left it.

* * * *

WILLY

The dispatcher said it was a domestic disturbance. By the time Officer Wilson arrived things had gotten more intense and much more complicated. A twenty-three-year-old man had a gun and was in his bedroom. He was threatening to kill himself.

The Stoddards were an immigrant couple. They had come to this country as young adults, had worked hard and had accomplished much by their standards. The farm was small, but they lived frugally and quite independently. The Stoddards still retained some of their old-world accent and manner of speech. They also retained certain attitudes about parental rights and the duties of their children.

Mr. and Mrs. Stoddard were angry. It was their "boy," and Mrs. Stoddard volunteered that she was ready to just go on up and talk to him about this "foolishness." Wilson's immediate thought was that this was the last kind of help he or the "boy" needed.

Wilson's district was "lonely," in that it was sparsely populated and distant from Sheriff's headquarters. It also meant that he could seldom count on "cover," or that it might, at best, be a long time in coming. He was, therefore, fairly self-reliant and took pride in handling most situations on his own. In this case, however, he recognized that any further activity on his own would be not only foolhardy but professionally irresponsible.

To have returned to the squad car to radio would have meant a later reentry into a bad situation. Entry being, in Wilson's mind, the riskier part of any call, he sought to avoid duplicating this risk when he could. He told the Stoddards to stay right there in their own living room for the time being. Not wanting to leave the house in case people moved or the situation deteriorated still further, he asked to use their phone.

Wilson explained the situation to his sergeant, who advised him to keep things stable if he could, and assured him that there would be support on the way. There was still no noise from upstairs. Under the circumstances Wilson figured the more he knew of what led up to the present situation the better.

"First, if we're going to be talking with your son, we should know his name. What does he generally go by?"

"Willy," said Mr. Stoddard.

"Yes," said Mrs. Stoddard, "that's what we call him." The Stoddards went on to explain how the whole thing had come about. Willy was "dumb," and just could not seem to do anything right. No matter how much they had struggled with him, he would still end up pulling some "stupid trick."

The last thing had to do with his having taken his father's truck. It was not in good condition, but it had been useful around the farm. Willy had disappeared with the truck several weeks ago and had come back three days ago without it. Willy had done some trading. Through a series of trades, and they were not sure how, he had managed to end up with a blanket. It was not losing the truck but seeing that damned blanket that really "burned" the old man. It rankled him, and he got a little angrier every time he thought about it. "A son of mine so God damned dumb a Cub Scout could have skinned him." He would rather the boy had wrecked the truck or even sold it and drunk the money up.

Mrs. Stoddard had never expected too much more from Willy. Her attitude and her behavior toward him had not changed much since he was nine. She continued to nag and complain as she always had. In any case things had become bad these last few days and had gotten a little worse today.

Mr. Stoddard felt a little better after explaining to Officer Wilson, and finally was able to say in a philosophical and resigned way, "I guess Willy has just never had very much on the ball."

The sergeant and two other officers arrived. Wilson explained the present situation, and they discussed alternatives and their various options. The sergeant suggested that he himself might talk with the man.

Wilson did not like the idea. The sergeant was taking over his call. He thought the sergeant was out of line, but he also knew that this was a man it did not pay to argue with. "Hell, if the sergeant wanted to play supercop, let him."

The sergeant moved carefully up the stairs and stood at the top where he could look down the hallway to the right and still be protected by the wall. He called out, "Willy, we'd like to talk with you." The only response was a muffled shot and the sound of the falling body.

Willy botched this too. The bullet had gone into his head but not fatally. The ambulance man, with patience and effort, got him down the narrow stairway. As the man was being carried out, Wilson heard his only words spoken, "Don't anyone ever call me Willy."

Both of these last two cases are of violence or the potential for such. It is one of the factors that separates the police caseload from all others. The officer's obligation to help is tempered by additional responsibilities to protect life, maintain peace and safeguard others in the process.

No other profession helps so many people who are as hostile or antagonistic to such aid, nor are other professionals frequently at such personal risk.

As with the case of Willy, the officers may proceed carefully and well only to have their best efforts fail. This must be accepted as a part of the job. There are no guaranteed results to any human interaction. There are sound procedures, but these, too, are subject to individual variability.

The individual, at best, can only surmise how another is hearing them or interpreting their actions. When the other person is mentally disorganized or under severe stress, the individual's capacity to surmise correctly is even further diminished.

SUMMARY

1. *The Police Caseload exists:* The documentation by these case examples is, at best, limited. Only the tip of an iceberg is presented. Police service, as the authors have personally experienced, extends into many areas of human stress and pain. By the very nature of police work, the officer is most likely to be one of the earliest helpers on the scene of many crisis situations.

2. *Diversity:* The authors have attempted to picture something of the diversity of contacts in police service calls. The request for service may be clear and direct or hidden. The need for help may not even be understood or wanted by the person in trouble. The recognition of such need by an officer, and the providing of even minimal help at an early stage, however, can be extremely significant. Opportunities for service exist in many calls.

3. *Complexity:* There are no clear, magical solutions. There

are good procedures to be understood, mastered and modified by common sense and the nature of the problem encountered. It is for this reason that the authors recommend training. Many of the skills and operational procedures of the mental health profession-al can be learned and adapted to police service problems. The techniques used in each case should be those which exhibit the most positive approach to each situation.

4. *Crime Prevention:* The authors would suggest that police service may well be the prime arena from which to consider crime prevention. Emotionally and socially dysfunctional individuals are in a large part made so by their environment. Identifying the life situations from which these people come, intervening where possible and diminishing damage to a developing generation are all within the scope of police work. It may be long range but certainly preventive in nature.

5. *The Dysfunctional Population:* Within the area of police service a large component of an "acting-out" or "action-oriented" population has been noted. This group represents the explosive and behavior-problem people. They are often helped only in the presence of their problem, and the police officer is the one most likely to be called. Once identified, patience and consis-tency on the part of the officer cannot be too highly recom-mended. Establishing boundaries for such people is therapeutic and may well be the only treatment they receive.

6. *Community Resources:* The community's social services do not cooperate well with the police system in its provision of ser-vice. Neither trusts nor respects the other. Police service is most often requested during those periods when the social services of a community are closed. This leaves the officer to cope as best as he can without such resources or support. Information is seldom shared by either officer or social agency, and so referrals are not made even where appropriate.

Regarding the six factors of the existence of police service, its diversity and complexity, preventive aspects, the "acting-out" population, and the inadequacy of community support services, there are many possible directions which will be considered for change in the following chapters.

Questions for Discussion

1. What is a caseload?
2. Does it make sense to speak of a police caseload?
3. As the authors describe police service, do you see it as a legitimate part of a police officer's job?
4. What techniques or skills do you think would help an officer in more effectively handling domestic disturbance calls?
5. What points do the authors make on an officer's approach to psychotics?
6. What are the possible advantages to the police system in more intensive work in juvenile problems?
7. What guidelines do the authors provide for recognizing and coping with sociopathic personalities?
8. How important is alcohol abuse in the police caseload?

Chapter III

TRAINING POLICE TO BETTER
HANDLE THEIR CASELOADS

TEACHING can be a lot of fun. After all, who would not enjoy spouting a few words of one's own wisdom and having a group of attentive students religiously gobbling up the pearls? It makes one feel important, as if one really is "somebody." Everybody ought to try teaching some of the things he knows from time to time. It is a good ego massage.

The authors' experience with police teaching has not always been quite that way. If one of us (the authors) wants to create a little anxiety in the other, it is only necessary to mention a few of our endeavors during our first year of operation. Then what it is like to be an outsider trying to gain some measure of acceptance into another system was fully experienced: the folly of the "experts" trying to impart some of their supposed expertise to a group that they did not understand and that saw little use for them. "Only a policeman can understand what it is like to be a policeman," is a statement we heard over and over again.

One fellow very aggressively pursued the authors to begin the rather tedious training which would qualify them to be police reservists during off-hours. "Then," he said, "we might listen a little bit."

"But we still won't be real policemen," the authors said.

"That's right," he countered. "And that's why we'll only listen a little bit. But at least we'll listen."

Quite seriously, the authors still have an occasional bad dream about some of the situations we found ourselves in that first year. Everyone, including the authors, has some need for love, for acceptance, and at times, that need in ourselves was squelched quite brutally. Policemen are not too tolerant of "outsiders" trying to tell them how to do their job. The fear and the anger this generates can often be quite intense. Some examples of this will be

44

given shortly. But first let us review some of the material already presented.

Thus far the point has been made that the police do have a caseload, just as the mental health professional in his office has a caseload. Of course, the police caseload is in many ways a more difficult one to deal with than that encountered by the average office-bound mental health professional.

As it is, the police do not do a bad job of handling their caseload. In the opening chapter, for example, the police involved did a creditable job of settling the immediate crisis involving the paranoid man and his neighbor. So someone might say, "Why not just let the police alone? They're doing okay their way. You folks stay in your offices and let them continue to do things the way they have been."

The authors will not counter this argument by giving examples of how a particular situation might have been handled better by the police. One could go into any field and find numerous examples of how things might be improved. Anyone completely satisfied with the *status quo* probably will not derive much benefit from reading this book any further. Perhaps satisfaction with the *status quo* makes the most sense. But the authors want more.

The goal is that of excellence. Everyone would like to see his community have the finest possible police force. Who would not like to see the police officer on the street give the best possible service to his caseload? This would mean that he would be well versed in human behavior, and that he would have a broad understanding of the present and future implications of his interactions with his clients. He would understand where he fits in as part of a wider service system, and he would be comfortable in utilizing other areas of that system for the betterment of the client.

Everyone would also like to see the police have a better feeling about the service aspects of their jobs. Most social workers are well aware that the police are often frustrated and angry over demands that are placed upon them for which they feel they have inadequate training and support. In the opening chapter, for example, the story of the police officer who picked up the man wandering in the street and then was subsequently turned away from the hospital emergency room was related. This officer was frustrated first because he did not understand why the resident did not accept the man, and then he was frustrated because he did not know what to do with him.

Is it important to be concerned about this officer's frustration? Is it unrealistic to talk of improving police service to their clients and of giving police more support in the management of their caseload? Is this of low priority in terms of other local and national needs? That will have to be decided by others than the authors, namely the people who buy programs such as the one developed by them.

Another very legitimate question at this point is whether or not mental health people really have anything to offer police in helping them manage their caseloads. Perhaps they might do more harm than good by dabbling in police affairs. Certainly mental health people have much to learn from police, but can they teach the police anything? It is hoped that, as this book progresses, the authors will be able to demonstrate their belief that they do have something to offer.

If one accepts the idea that police could use a little help and that mental health people can help, then two immediate avenues come to mind. One approach would be to give police more training in accepted human behavioral techniques. Another would be to develop a program where police and behavioral specialists could work alongside each other in formal collaboration, so that a mental health professional might interject himself in those police situations where it seems appropriate.

The authors have worked in both of these directions. In Chapters IV and V will be found discussions of experiments with the police social worker. In this chapter the text will focus on attempts to share with police some views about people and their problems.

When human behavioral training for police is discussed, the name of Morton Bard has to be considered as foremost. His work in New York, originally focusing on family disturbance calls, demonstrated both the need for and the efficacy of teaching crisis intervention techniques to police officers.[1] Since the publicizing

---

[1]Bard, M.: *Family Crisis Intervention: From Concept to Implementation.* U.S. Department of Justice, Law Enforcement Assistance Administration, National Institute of Law Enforcement and Criminal Justice, Washington, D.C., December, 1973.

of his work around 1970, there have been numerous programs in different parts of the country trying various approaches to police training, all of which were patterned after Mr. Bard's original work.

The program being used in Portland, Oregon, is but one adaptation of Bard's initial ideas. While much credit should be given to Bard's initial impetus, it must be said that some further contributions have been made by others in this burgeoning field.

We have been extensively involved in police training for four and one half years. Both metropolitan and rural police have been trained, from the recruit to the captain level. We have worked with corrections officers, police community relations officers, police reservists, university security officers, police dispatchers, various types of civilian police personnel, and college students in police science. In terms of numbers, significant contact has been made with perhaps a thousand such individuals.

Work with the experienced street officer was found to be most gratifying. Once the officer begins to trust the teacher and brings his rich experience into the various training sessions, interesting meetings are often the result.

Our training modalities have been varied, and we have undergone much trial and error learning. In general, it has been found that the most successful learning experiences are those in which the student is somehow involved in activities where he has to *do* something, to share in the responsibility.

One mainstay of our training has been a five-day, forty-hour seminar entitled *Understanding People*. A highlight of these seminars has consisted of field trips to various mental health agencies, where the participants experience supervised interaction with agency clients. Twenty-seven of these successful seminars have been completed, with a total attendance of about 360 people. Much of this chapter will be devoted to a description of these seminars as they, more than anything else, epitomize the most desired training techniques. Before getting into this, however, the authors would like to relate, in more general terms, some of their experiences.

In our efforts to learn about police and to make ourselves

known to them, we have been very willing to try different things. In our first years we spent many hours riding in patrol cars. We also became involved in some training activities that in retrospect were not such good ideas. Some examples of our failures follow.

Imagine yourself before a group of sixty policemen, many of them older and cynical, most armed, some in civilian dress and some in uniforms. You are meeting with them in a huge concrete structure that is part armory and part bomb shelter. There are no windows. These sixty men are between you and the door. You have just been introduced as a mental health professional who will be with them for the next six hours of this in-service school. You are to somehow talk with them about understanding people.

Your introduction is greeted with some snickering and an uneasy shuffling of chairs and feet. You tell them a little about yourself, and then ask if there are some areas they might like to talk about with you. There is just sullen silence. Then you ask for the names of some of the men, trying to establish rapport.

"You're not going to write our names down, are you?" someone asks, quite concerned.

"I thought I might," you answer matter of factly.

"What will you do with the paper they're written on?" the voice further asks.

"What is it you're concerned about?"

"I don't want my name to get into the wrong hands."

"What would be the wrong hands?" you ask.

"The hippies and the other freaks who want a revolution. If there is a revolution the police will be the first to get it. I don't want my name as a policeman written in too many places."

You try to hold back a laugh as you think you are being kidded. You survey the scene and study the man speaking. He is not joking, you decide. He is serious about his fear. Then your legs begin to quake a little as your own fear is stirred up. You have a few minutes less than six hours to go, and you actually wonder if you will make it out of this tomb-like structure in one piece.

You brought some films with you. You brought them because they had supposedly been successfully used in police training elsewhere. They are a series of short vignettes of police handling difficult situations. One shows a policeman rather roughly arresting a black. Another shows police being hassled by some long haired youngster. The point of the films is to stimulate discussion, to help the police to open up about their feelings. You decide to show one of the films, hoping to loosen up the group a bit.

You try to explain the purpose of the film, and then you show it. After it is finished you turn on the lights and the faces look even angrier.

"That's a film critical of police," one man says. "No good policeman would act like that. Where did you get that film? You shouldn't be showing it around. That gives police a bad image."

You explain again that the film is used to stimulate discussion, not necessarily to criticize police. A few people seem to understand, mostly the younger ones, and it seems as if there is a bit of support for you. Some people try to get into an honest discussion of the film, but others heckle them down, stating that the film was a disgrace to the police and was completely unrealistic.

Somehow, gamely, as real proof of your own mental health, you survive the six hours. You even feel as if you have established some good communication with some of the men, and you have seen some of them open up new lines of communication with each other, as they realize that they are not alone in their fears and frustrations and anguish. But on the whole the group remained cooly distant. "Just what is the point of your being here?" one man asked near the end. "Only police can understand police. If you want to know what it's *really* all about, join the force for awhile. Then maybe we'll listen to you."

You leave completely drained, but not very relieved, for you have committed yourself to eleven more of these sessions, each with a different group.

The authors have been involved in a situation like the one just described. It was painful but not without some learning value. We learned of the isolation of police and their mistrust of outsiders. We also relearned what we already knew — sixty is much too large a group to work with effectively, and six hours is not nearly long enough to begin to break through the resistance.

A second example of failure in communication between police and teacher may be seen in the following:

> You have been asked to give a three-hour presentation on mental health to a statewide police academy, where recruits from some very tiny departments, maybe having only two members, are present. Some of the students are college graduates while some have barely finished high school. While preparing your lecture, someone on the staff of the academy warns you that it will be a hard job.
>
> "You'll have to work hard to make it relevant," he says. "Some of these people are pretty narrow. Once I got up to talk about jails, and one of them said he didn't want to learn anything about jails. I asked him why not, and he said that his town didn't have a jail and, therefore, he didn't need to know anything about them."
>
> With that bit of encouragement, you try anyhow. You meet the class of fifty people, again too large and for too brief a period of time, and try to engage them in a discussion. A few people respond, but most do not. You talk a bit about personality in general, and ask for some speculation about some of the characteristics of the police personality.
>
> "Loyalty," someone says.
>
> "What do you mean?" you ask.
>
> "I mean police stick together. One for all and all for one. It's us against them."
>
> "Who's *them?*"
>
> "The jerks. The people who aren't police."
>
> You very gently and tactfully try to point out that not all nonpolice are "jerks," and that there are some dangers in the sort of clannish attitude he is espousing.
>
> Immediately you are attacked from all sides. "See what we mean," someone says. "You just don't understand."
>
> One fellow becomes quite agitated and denounces you as a "silly liberal." You lose your temper a bit, and you tell him that he's acting dumb. The situation deteriorates, and soon nothing you say is being heard. You finish your session. After it is over one of the students introduces himself as a college graduate. "I felt sorry for you," he says. "These guys are really something else. You'll never get through out here."
>
> You don't believe him, and you think there has to be a way.

You revise your approach and try again. The same thing happens. You try different things. You ask for more time, then less time, then more time. You have a policeman friend accompany you to do a little blocking for you and to convince the class that you're not a complete fool and what you say has a bit of merit.

At the end of each academy class, there is an evaluation of the different blocks of instruction. Always you get awful, often angry evaluations. Finally, after two years of this, you quit.

Again, there is something to be learned. No matter what is endeavored, some situations are impossible. Better to avoid them in the first place. But how can anyone know that in advance unless they try? Perhaps the lesson in humility will be helpful, at least.

One last failure before looking at some successful attempts at communication.

You have been asked by a local police department to help them with a problem they are having with the black community. Most of the officers are white, and they are having a lot of trouble dealing with the small but increasingly vocal black population. You suggest a series of meetings between the white officers and some blacks, hoping that maybe you can facilitate communication and increase understanding. Both sides are reluctant.

"It won't do any good," one black says. "Whitey will never listen to us. Somehow we will end up with the short end of it."

"What's there to learn about blacks? They should learn about us," an officer says with disdain.

"Will the cops have their guns with them?" a black asks. "If they do, we'll bring ours too."

You work hard, soothing and reassuring, compromising about who will and who will not bring guns, and finally you set up a three-day workshop to be attended by eight blacks and eight officers.

The big day arrives, and you're very nervous. You arrive at the meeting place and the blacks begin to trickle in, surly and guarded, but at least there. No officers show. After two hours you make some phone calls. You reach a high police official, "Sorry, we had to call that off," he says. "Didn't someone notify you? We have a lot of men on sick leave this week, and there might be some trouble in the black community, so we can't spare anybody. Let's try again some other time."

You break the news to the blacks, who do not seem as surprised as you. "Like I said, we always come out on the short end," one says. "Whitey never keeps his word. Now maybe you'll begin to believe it too."

You are supported by them, and they really seem to appreciate your efforts, and in this uneducated group of men you feel a sensitivity and compassion that you have seldom felt in a police group. You spend the three days with them anyhow, minus the officers, and you learn a lot. Once again the failure is hardly a total loss. You find that you, too, are quite a racist but maybe a little less so after these three days. You also learn that you have a lot more to learn in preparing people for the challenge of the little confrontations you dream up.

There have been many more failures than these, but these seem to stand out. Of course, there have been successes too. Without them, there would be nothing to write about.

The authors feel that the ideal situation would be one in which we would be allowed to work intensely for a period of years with a group of police to make them into mental health specialists who could become trainers and resource people for the department. It now appears that the program has finally evolved to that point. This will be discussed in the final chapter.

Initially the police were unwilling to make that kind of commitment, so we were forced to come up with something less demanding. The five-day seminar, which was billed as an introduction to human behavior and entitled *Understanding People,* was the tool chosen to gain some initial acceptance. A five-day commitment was limited enough so that the police were not too threatened by the idea. And it did not demand that much time. However, it was intensive enough so that the two groups could really get to know each other. While it was doubtful that many specific techniques or skills could be imparted in such a short time, it was felt that perhaps an attitude that emphasized a feeling of understanding rather than judgement could be conveyed.

As stated earlier, twenty-seven such seminars have now been given. These have been attended by about 360 people in all. The usual seminar size has been from twelve to fifteen students. At times a seminar involves people from only one department, while at other times people from various departments may become involved.

These seminars have been extensively evaluated, and these evaluations will be discussed at the end of this chapter. In general, the seminars have been well received and have accomplished the purposes of gaining acceptance into the police system and imparting some positive attitudes about human behavior. This is well summed up by what was said recently by a police captain while discussing the intensive training program involving police and mental health care workers. "Everybody accepts you guys now. We've all heard what you've had to say, and it makes sense. Nobody gets uptight now, like they did four years ago when they hear talk about social work and crisis intervention and stuff like that."

The basic model for the seminars was borrowed from the Menninger Foundation in Topeka, Kansas, where first Harry Levinson and then Herbert Klemme have long conducted week-long seminars entitled *Toward Understanding Man* for the executives of industry. The National Training Laboratory Institute of Applied Behavioral Science, headquartered in Washington, D. C., has also used a similar week-long model in training various groups.

These seminars generally combine three elements: (1) a somewhat informal didactic portion, with emphasis on basic concepts of human behavior and communication skills, and including many experiential exercises; (2) field trips to local mental health facilities, where police tour the facility, meet the staff, and conduct supervised interviews with agency clients; (3) daily discussion groups which are small enough to allow ventilation of feelings, interchange of ideas and some experiential learning of group process.*

The physical facilities for the seminars are less than ideal but they are adequate. Most of the teaching is done in one room, while another serves as the main office. Having two rooms permits the

---

*The illustration schedule (Table I) at the end of this chapter provides a format for a typical seminar week.

separation of participants for small group discussions.

During Monday's orientation each participant, in civilian dress, is provided with a name tag and a copy of the schedule. The attempt is made to put everyone on a first-name basis. On this occasion *only* will everyone wait up to fifteen minutes for stragglers before starting. A fairly complete introduction of everyone, including the leaders, is encouraged in a "going around the room" manner. A tone of informality is established without giving up either authority or responsibility for the seminar.

The history and purpose of the seminars is explained, and the weekly schedule is gone over. Anxiety is usually high on this first day, and we try to alleviate as much of it as possible by being quite concrete and specific. We also go into detail regarding such things as the location of the rest rooms and the parking situation. Questions are encouraged again and again.

Then the participants are divided into two pairs of groups, one pair for small group discussions and one pair for field trips. In the former strangers are encouraged to group, while in the latter, because of the realities of car pools and such, convenience is the standard.

Mental Health I consists of a worksheet asking for definitions of the people in the field of mental health and asking a few basic questions such as "What is mental health?" Participants are paired with strangers if possible, and they are asked to go over the worksheet together. Then the entire group goes over the worksheet.

In this and all subsequent exercises, large sheets of inexpensive newsprint are used by us to note, with a crayon or felt pen, key points. The newsprint sheets are easily transferred from an easel to the wall, where they are taped for the duration of the seminar, to trace its week-long history.

On Monday morning a brief outline for interviewing patients is also presented, with a focus on the upcoming field trips.

On Monday afternoon, with a format including brief lectures, role playing by the staff, handouts and exercises, the basic communication skills of behavior description, paraphrase and perception check are presented. These are partially discussed in Miles' book on groups.[2]

Then a staff member conducts an interview of a class member, if one is willing, or another staff member. This demonstration interview serves as a model of the techniques discussed and of the information gathering process.

The day ends with two small group discussions, each led by a staff member.

In the illustration schedule Tuesday begins with a lecture and discussion of psychopaths. Wide-ranging topics, such as delinquency, suicide and the problems of blacks and other minority groups, have been presented here or elsewhere in the seminar.

In the communication exercise subgroups of three follow a written guideline to reinforce their understanding of the three aspects of communication presented on Monday afternoon.

A long lunch break is provided because of the additional time needed for travelling to the location of the field trip.

In the illustration schedule field trips are scheduled for the psychiatric crisis unit of the county hospital, for the local state mental hospital and for the main office of the county mental health clinic. Depending on the composition of the group, other settings have been used. For corrections officers from the county jail, for example, the juvenile detention home has been used in place of the mental health clinic.

These field trips always cause a lot of anxiety for the participants, but they are usually the highlights of the week. Depending upon the availability of clients willing to be interviewed, the availability of staff and the availability of such things as one-way mirrors, a variety of grouping formats have been used. Always, however, there is emphasis on involving the participants in supervised interviews with agency clients. Trainers are present on these trips, but the major responsibility is delegated to someone within the agency. One officer made the interesting observation that the field trips are similar to a police call. In each case the officer rather tensely drives someplace in his car, knowing that he will be called upon to perform when he reaches his destination.

---

[2]Miles, M.: *Learning to Work in Groups.* New York, Columbia University Teachers College Press, 1965.

Wednesday morning begins with some sharing of experiences by the two groups about their field trips. Then mental health workers move into Mental Health II, which is a worksheet similar to Mental Health I, but this time the program involves the common clinical syndromes. A short lecture on commonly abused drugs follows, before the third small group session and the afternoon field trip.

Thursday morning is devoted to a game called Star Power which involves the participants in competitive interaction with each other and eventually in a three-tiered society.[3] Authority, power, risk and social mobility are all experienced. This usually brings out a lot of feelings, and a discussion of these is the last stage of the game. This discussion usually carries into the small groups.

In the afternoon there is a reversal of the Tuesday afternoon visits.

On Friday morning one of the trainers discusses actual case material from his forensic psychiatry experiences. Using what they have learned throughout the week, participants are encouraged to try to understand the criminal behavior presented. Then they are urged to change roles and to try to view the material from various vantage points, such as the court, society, the subject and the psychiatrist.

On this last day a catered lunch is provided by the staff. This is the only time during the week that everyone involved in the seminar eats together.

On Friday afternoon the participants are involved in an application exercise. Each is asked to consider policy or procedural changes he might make in his agency if he were given the chief's job and a mandate for improvement in the service aspects of police work. The group is broken into subgroups to work on this, and the reports are later made to the entire group for a critique.

Then each participant is given a diploma, and is told that this training is approved for credit by the State Board of Police Standards and Training. It is also announced that this week will be

---

[3]Shirts, R.: *Star Power*, as modified by Lohman A., Lohman J., and Lohman M. Available through Simile II, P.O. Box 1023, LaJolla, California, 92037.

accepted as an elective course at the local community college if anyone is interested in applying there for the credit.

After a last small group discussion, which deals primarily with the issues of loss and termination, each participant completes an anonymous questionnaire concerning the course. These questionnaires constitute an evaluation of the mental health workers, and are freely available to anyone interested in the program.

With the completion of the questionnaire, the seminar is officially over. The staff is available to talk informally, however, for anyone who wants to linger on. This, on occasion, runs into the evening hours.

It should be noted that flexibility is required during these seminars. The trainers should be willing to deviate from the planned schedule if something unscheduled seems to be more profitable for the group at the moment.

As these seminars have been developed, it has become apparent that some basic principles are necessary for success. These basic principles are really extensions of lessons learned from clinical work with individuals. They might be summarized as follows: (1) always stay at the understanding level of the participants; (2) challenge in a low-level way but not so vigorously as to increase defensiveness; (3) offer a wide range of learning experiences, so that each person will find something to which he can relate.

Regarding the first principle, since mental health workers are not experts in police work, it is difficult at times to know where the participants (police) stand emotionally and intellectually. To emphasize the desire to learn about the police, we do ride in patrol cars and spend time visiting the local jails. This has helped us to appreciate how an officer must feel in a setting — such as on a hospital ward — which is familiar to the mental health worker. It is felt that anyone working with a different culture, whether it includes teachers, ministers or nurses, must demonstrate both to himself and to that group some willingness to risk by making some sort of foray into that seemingly alien world.

Also, when confronted with gaps in our understanding about police work, we try to make this into an advantage. Through us the police can see themselves as others might see them. The authors point out that the police will have to work hard during the week to extract from their interaction with us something that will have meaning and value for them. The mental health worker presents his viewpoints, and it is the task of the police to make these viewpoints relevant for themselves.

At the beginning both sides are anxious. It is, at times, tempting for us to turn off the anxious police attacks upon us by taking a popular stand, or by enjoying a joke at someone else's expense, or by pretending to understand clearly something that is ambiguous. Mental health workers must constantly keep themselves honest by reminding each other that they are there to serve the needs of the participants and not primarily for their own personal needs for recognition and love. Criticism especially is encouraged, in order to air any negative feelings. With these difficulties in mind, it is important that any such seminars involve at least two leaders to help each other.

In regard to low-level confrontation, we do not see ourselves as therapists but as human relations teachers. We see ourselves as presenting new material and challenging old beliefs and prejudices with an intensity somewhat short of that which would bring about group defensiveness and completely cut the mental health worker off from the police. This means that we often walk a real tightrope, since the group we are working with has a strong feeling against outsiders who supposedly do not know what it really is all about. The goal is to open the participants to new alternatives and options.

At times we have inadvertently pushed too hard and have really increased group defensiveness rather than alleviated it. An example of this involved a session on black problems.

During the first year of operation we were advised by participants that we should somehow focus on problems some of the police were having with the black community. To accomplish this a few exercises were developed and some blacks were invited in to meet with the group during one of the seminar mornings. The blacks were not radical, but they were encouraged to be honest about their feelings toward police. Regardless of their life situations, they all did have tales of being embarrassed at the hands of the police. Usually the police group would then close against the mental health workers and the black or blacks present, trying to convince all present that police were misunderstood. The group was urged to try to understand rather than debate with the black side, but this was usually to no avail.

The experience was often dismissed with the observation that the blacks interviewed were either "different" and, therefore, not relevant to the total black community; or it was said that the blacks were just spouting the standard, unfounded antipolice line. This seminar activity was finally discontinued since it was felt that such activity was reinforcing rather than diminishing bias.

Another area in which group defensiveness exhibited itself to the point of almost causing a discontinuance of a part of the program was in videotaped role-playing. Through a local community college, the program was able to utilize a very realistic set portraying either a store or a two-room house. Using acting students and some professional actors, we were able to set up typical police-human relations calls, such as an attempted suicide or "longhairs" causing a disturbance. Police would respond in teams of two to these various vignettes, the scenes were videotaped, and then the videotapes were played back for the entire group and discussed. At one time almost an entire seminar day was devoted to this activity.

The police often saw this as an attempt on the part of the mental health workers to show them up and to make them look bad, and they strongly criticized the whole thing as not being realistic. Once an officer claimed that he smelled marihuana on one of the actors, and there was some genuine discussion about a possible arrest.

Finally the idea was hit upon of having the police write the scripts and do the acting themselves. This minimized the role of the outsiders, and the activity was much better accepted. Many good lessons were then learned. One officer, for example, marvelled at what a tension release it had been for him to call a policeman "Pig!" Eventually this activity had to be discontinued when the facilities became unavailable.

In regard to offering a variety of learning experiences, some intellectual and some quite experiential, it is felt that the schedule speaks for itself. The value of the agency visits with actual patient contact cannot be overemphasized.

These programs have been hectic, though, with both police and agency staff expressing great concern at times. Agency staff have been concerned that the police presence, even in civilian dress, would destroy the agency's relationship with patients. There was concern that an interview with some police officers would cause harm to patients, who might see it as an attack on them. The authors have also been made aware of considerable prejudice against police, the "bad guys," among mental health people. We have tried to overcome this by pointing out time and again that, like it or not, police would have contact with patients on the street, and then the mental health workers would have no control whatsoever, except insofar as they were willing to work with police now.

The police were afraid of being put on the spot in front of their colleagues, and they were afraid, too, that they might harm the patients somehow. They also shared the common fear of "mentals."

In defense of the program, there have been from the outset police-patient interviews, and there has not thus far been any harm done to anyone as a result. Many patients, in fact, seem to have benefited, as they suddenly see police as being quite human.

One example in particular stands out. A lady came to the Mental Health Clinic in a very anxious and depressed state. For one hour she was interviewed by two officers and a social worker. One officer did most of the interviewing, and at the end of the interview he timidly asked her if she felt any different than when she came in. "Much, much better," she replied. That officer was walking on clouds as he repeated that comment over and over to anyone who would listen.

Objectively evaluating a training program that attempts to teach rather subtle interpersonal skills and effect some attitude change is a very difficult thing, especially when economic resources for evaluation are limited. Still, a number of different approaches have been tried and some things learned in the process.

At the end of each forty-hour seminar the participants were asked to write their impressions of the week. A sample of the type of questionnaire used is included at the end of this chapter. The first question is, "Was this course worth the time spent?" From a total of about 360 participants, only about ten have responded in a negative way to this question. Often this question is answered in very glowing positive terms. A frequent statement is to the effect that the training has given the student a new way of looking at things. In many ways the week's experience, with its group feeling, resembles a religious conversion.

After the first eighteen months of operation, the authors had a more elaborate evaluation of the forty-hour seminars done by Dr. Milton Davis, an industrial psychologist associated with Portland State University. This study consisted of two main parts.

The first part consisted of a structured interview and the completion of a standard questionnaire with 125 Multnomah County citizens who had recently had direct contact with Multnomah County deputy sheriffs. These contacts were for what were defined as service calls, especially those involving interpersonal crises such as attempted suicides, family fights, psychotic conditions and the like. The primary goal was to determine if the behavior of the deputy sheriffs who had received our training was any different from those who had not been trained. The final number of completed interviews and questionnaries involved sixty-two trained officers and sixty-three nontrained officers.

The police system has been described as a somewhat closed one where there is mistrust of outsiders. There is a constant defensiveness and fear of criticism. With this attitude it is not surprising that there was considerable hesitancy on the part of police officials authorizing this study. There was concern that going to a citizen and asking him how he felt about a recent police contact would open up a floodgate of criticism about the police system. The authors too, were a bit reluctant about the design of the study. They really doubted that one week's training would effect any measurable behavioral change, and it was felt that a finding of "no change" would be held against us. We were also worried that a barrage of citizen complaints about the police would somehow be blamed on the mental health workers involved in this program. Still it was decided to take a chance, since the idea was intriguing. No one had ever bothered to ask the local consumer how he felt about police service.

This part of the evaluation was limited to contacts made by those uniformed officers who were under thirty-five years of age and who had a college degree. These limitations were imposed to minimize influences other than the training experience.

The results of the study were surprising. Citizens interviewed had overwhelmingly positive things to say about the Multnomah County Sheriff's Department. Many were extremely pleased that anyone cared enough to ask about how they felt and praised the department highly on this score alone. From the training point of view, the study was disappointing. The citizen response was so uniformly positive that there was no significant difference between the untrained and trained officers. Mental health workers had expected a finding of no difference but were surprised to see how positively the citizenry viewed the police.

In general, the study was so pleasing to the police that few held the finding of no difference against us. We did react with openness and some disappointment and talked of improving the training. We did our best not to be defensive, and this helped our credibility. One of the departments that we had been working with and with which we had been having some difficulties did use this study as the rationale to discontinue sending people to the seminars, however.

Since it was not felt that the initial phase of this study answered all of the questions about the value and impact of training, a second phase was conducted. This second study was based upon reactions of police officers who had participated in the course. This was similar in respect to the brief questionnaire at the completion of the course, except that it was more extensive and separated from the course in time. Some of the officers had taken the course as much as sixteen months before the interview.

In this phase of the study 100 officers representing different departments and with varied backgrounds were interviewed. A questionnaire was developed which included both structured objective questions as well as more open-ended ones. A copy of this questionnaire is included at the end of this chapter.

This showed an overwhelming acceptance from police for the course. For example, the percentage of police officers who responded with a statement of *strongly agree* or *agree* to the following benefits received from attending the course is listed below:

Better understanding of people	89%
More knowledge about interviewing techniques	87%
Better self-understanding	84%
Better communication with citizens	83%
More self-confidence	71%
Better communication with fellow officers	67%

In answer to the question, "Should there be additional follow-up training courses offered in the subject matter?" 93 percent of the trainees said yes. This has led us into our latest endeavor, which is the intensive, long-term training that will be discussed in the last chapter.

One last evaluation of the program has been completed. After three years of existence, and after moving from federal funding to local county funding, another study was done by the county planning and evaluation section. A main purpose of this study was to determine whether there should be continued funding of the program, especially in the face of a local budget crunch. Using the questionnaire and interview techniques, the entire program, including the training and the service aspects which will be discussed in Chapters IV and V, was evaluated. Contacts were made with deputies, police administration and other agencies that the program interfaced with. The conclusions of this study were very flattering, and will be quoted in their entirety.

> Urban tensions are perhaps most intensely experienced by those whose responsibility it is to enforce the law and ensure a more cohesive social fabric. In recent years this onerous task has received much community disapprobation. Contrary to popular stereotype, much police work involves not arrests and investigative activities, but human relations work. (Johnson and Gregory, 1971). Police spend much of their time in social

work roles: settling disputes, counseling children, dealing with psychotic behavior.

Until recently these responsibilities were guided only by the seasoned experience which "many years on the force" may have afforded but certainly did not guarantee. To supplement this experience (often merely 'lucky' intuitive judgments), training programs, such as LECP, teach officers to manage disputants in a humane, helpful manner.

LECP training, whose efficacy is so highly acclaimed by participants, should be expanded in the immediate future. Simple, easily organized training activities may be offered at no greater cost in order to more effectively meet the needs of deputies who express a genuine desire to learn.

The necessity of having a professional social worker attached to a law enforcement agency has also been verified in this analysis by officers themselves. The merger of two distinctly different services could have easily resulted in role confusion, interprofessional jealously or resentment. Instead, it has produced a positive attitudinal change among the respective participants. The social worker has provided a new resource to the officers and, in so doing, helped improve their skills in the management of domestic disputes.

Regardless of how ingeniously designed and artfully carried out, no police or community relations program can hope to eliminate the social and psychological factors which require police intervention (President's Commission on Law Enforcement, 1967). However, as community professionals learn to mutually serve needful citizens, the severity of such problems may be reduced.

The Law Enforcement Counseling Program recognizes the very real pressures and highly sophisticated demands which daily face officers and seeks to transform their tension into intelligent, effective action. Support of such a program is a useful and necessary aspect of improving the community's law enforcement and social service to those who were, heretofore, ignored.

Despite the many problems inherent in any program such as this, the program has received enough encouragement to continue. The best encouragement has come from the officers themselves.

Questions for Discussion

1. Do you think you have to actually experience something to fully understand it?
2. Could you outline a course of instruction teaching something you know well to a group that does not know it?
3. What are some of the elements of a good teacher?
4. How long does it usually take for trust to develop between two people or two systems?
5. How can you evaluate attitude change?
6. What do mental health professionals have to teach to police?
7. Does it make more sense to have every officer in a police department receive extensive training in human behavior rather than to have only a few departmental specialists in crisis intervention?
8. In terms of the spending of tax dollars, where should the training of police in human behavior be ranked with the community's other needs?

(Illustration Schedule)

UNDERSTANDING PEOPLE SEMINAR
Law Enforcement Counseling
May 21-25, 1973

Staff:

Charles Fosterling, M.S.W., M.P.H., Project Director
Edward Colbach, M.D., Psychiatric Consultant
James Euler, M.S.W., Law Enforcement Counselor
Lynda Broadhead, Administrative Assistant

Monday	Tuesday	Wednesday	Thursday	Friday
9:00 - 9:45 Introduction and Orientation	9:00 - 10:00 Psychopaths	9:00 - 9:30 Debriefing	9:00 - 11:00 Star Power	9:00 - 12:00 Forensic Psychiatry
9:45 Coffee Break		9:30 - 10:15 Mental Health II		(Coffee Break) (10:30 - 11:00)
10:00 - 12:00 Mental Health I	10:00 - 11:00 Exercise in Communication	10:15 Coffee Break	11:00 Coffee Break	
	11:00 Coffee Break	10:30 - 11:15 Drugs and Withdrawal Symptoms		
12:00 - 1:00 Lunch Break	11:15 - 12:00 Small Groups (discussion)	11:15 - 12:00 Small Groups (discussion)	11:15 - 12:00 Small Groups (discussion)	12:00 - 1:00 Group Lunch, provided by staff
1:00 - 1:45 Behavior Description	12:00 - 1:30 Lunch Break	12:00 - 1:30 Lunch Break	12:00 - 1:30 Lunch Break	1:00 - 2:30 Application Exercise
1:45 Coffee Break				2:30 Coffee Break
2:00 - 3:30 Paraphrase and Perception Check				
3:30 - 4:00 Demonstration Interview	1:30 - 5:00 *Group A* – Crisis Unit of Multnomah County Hospital – See Liz Washington, R.N.	1:30 - 5:00 *Groups A and B* Dammasch State Hospital Wilsonville See Ms. Gaynelle Alfred, M.S.W.	1:30 - 5:00 *Group A.* – Mental Health Clinic – 12240 N.E. Glisan See Bill Kruger, M.S.W.	2:45 - 3:30 Small Groups (discussion)
4:00 Coffee Break	*Group B* – Mental Health Clinic – 12240 N.E. Glisan See Bill Kruger, M.S.W.		*Group B.* – Crisis Unit of Multnomah County Hospital – See Liz Washington, R.N.	3:30 - 4:30 Written Evaluation
4:15 - 5:00 Small Groups (discussion)				

Evaluation Filled Out at End of Each Seminar

UNDERSTANDING PEOPLE SEMINAR

Evaluation Questionnaire

March 11-15, 1974

Please explain answers:

1) Was this seminar worth the time spent?

2) What was most helpful to you?

3) What was least helpful to you?

4) What did you think of the following:

    a) Mental Health I?

    b) Mental Health II?

    c) Mental Health III?

    d) Film on alcohol problems (The Mask)?

    e) Discussion following the film?

5) What were your impressions of the following:

    a) Visit to Dammasch State Hospital?

    b) Visit to Crisis Unit?

    c) Visit to Juvenile Court?

    d) Visit to Mental Health Clinic?

6) How could this seminar have been more helpful to you?

7) Please note any additional comments you wish to make?
    (use reverse side of sheet also)

Citizen Interview Regarding Their Reactions to Police

NORTHWEST PSYCHOLOGICAL SERVICES

FAMILY CRISIS PROJECT

Date:_____

Interviewer:_____

Case:_____

IDENTIFICATION INFORMATION

DISPATCHER   OFFICER

Date call   Time   Time   Time
Received_____   Received_____ Arrived_____ Closed_____

Name of person who called:_____ Telephone No._____

Address of incident:_____

Type of incident:_____

Officers:_____

Additional back-up:_____

Type: Trained_____

Not Trained_____

Officer and Social Worker_____

Other_____

Interviewee: Person who made call:_____

Person who caused call:_____

Observer:_____

When the officer arrived what happened?_____

_____

_____

_____

_____

_____

A_____ S_____ R_____ C_____

O_____ S E_____

Rev. 2-11/17/71

In order to record your opinions and feelings, I will ask you a number of questions about the Officer's behavior. First, I would like to ask you some questions with which you may disagree strongly, merely disagree, express no feeling either way, merely agree, or strongly agree.

	DS	D	N	A	SA
He introduced himself politely and clearly.	—	—	—	—	—
He was polite and respectful to those present.	—	—	—	—	—
He demonstrated understanding of the problems presented.	—	—	—	—	—
He helped to calm down those people who were there.	—	—	—	—	—
He maintained self-control at all times.	—	—	—	—	—
He was nonthreatening to those present.	—	—	—	—	—
He conducted himself in a professional or gentlemanlike manner.	—	—	—	—	—
He appeared nervous or unsure of himself.	—	—	—	—	—
He got angry, used swear words and was abusive.	—	—	—	—	—

All right, let's look at the officers conduct in a few different ways. In this case you need answer only "yes" or "no" and I may request additional information.

Did you feel that the officer handled the situation properly? Yes__ No__

Why?_____

_____

_____

Did the officer take sides? Yes__ No__ Was he objective in doing so? Yes__ No__

Should he have remained impartial? Yes__ No__

Did the officer make any suggestions that might help prevent similar situations?

Yes__ No__ If yes, what suggestions did he offer?_____

_____

Was an arrest made? Yes__ No__

Did you feel that this arrest was necessary? Yes__ No__

Did the officer handle it properly? Yes__ No__

If yes, explain_____

_____

Did the officer use more physical force than was justified?   Yes__ No__

If yes, explain_____

In general, how do you feel about the quality of the police and deputy sheriffs service available to you?

Excellent   ____   _____
Very good   ____   _____
Satisfactory ____   _____
Rather Poor   ____   _____
Very Poor   ____   _____

In the last five years, how many official contacts have you had?   _____

In conclusion I would like to have you express your opinions or any general feelings that you have about this particular situation as to how it was handled. I would also be interested in knowing any suggestions that you have about how these law enforcement people could be of greater service to you.

_____

_____

_____

_____

_____

_____

_____

_____

_____

_____

_____

_____

_____

_____

_____

_____

_____

_____

Thank you very much for your time and courtesy. As I have indicated earlier, we are

interested in learning how to improve the quality of law enforcement services to you.

Follow-up Interview of Police Officers Who Completed Seminar

APPENDIX A

NORTHWEST PSYCHOLOGICAL SERVICES

FAMILY CRISIS TRAINING EVALUATION

Date:_____

Interviewer:_____

Case Number:_____

Present Duty Assignment:_____ Age:_____

*Years of Police Experience:*_____

Date Completed Course:_____ Years of Formal Education:_____

1. Have you been able to apply what you learned from this course: (a) In your
    official duties with citizens? Yes_____ No_____. How specifically?

    _____

    _____

    _____

    _____

    (b) In your relationships with other police officers? Yes_____ No_____.
    How specifically?

    _____

    _____

    _____

    _____

    (c) In your own personal life? Yes_____ No_____. How specifically?

    _____

    _____

    _____

    _____

2. Are there any improvements you would recommend to the course? (Explain)

    _____

    _____

    _____

    _____

3. The following are possible benefits that people may have received from the FCU
    Training Project - "UNDERSTANDING PEOPLE SEMINAR." We are interested in your
    degree of agreement regarding each of the following items:

	Strongly Disagree	Dis-agree	Neutral	Agree	Strongly Agree	Not Applicable
I received the following bene-fits from attending this course						
(a) Better understanding of people	____	____	____	____	____	____
(b) Increased self-assurance	____	____	____	____	____	____
(c) More self-confidence	____	____	____	____	____	____
(d) More knowledge about interviewing techniques	____	____	____	____	____	____
(e) Better communication with fellow officers	____	____	____	____	____	____
(f) Better communication with citizens	____	____	____	____	____	____

Other:_____

_____

_____

4. The following are activities that have been used in various training sessions.
    We are interested in knowing your reactions to each of:

I feel this way about:	Very Unfavorable	Somewhat Unfavorable	Neutral	Favor-able	Very Favorable	Not Applicable
(a) SLEE Lab.	____	____	____	____	__ __	____
(b) Small group discussions	____	____	____	____	__ __	____
(c) Crisis Unit	____	____	____	____	____	____
(d) Follow-up sessions	____	____	____	____	____	____
(e) Value of films	____	____	____	____	____	____
(f) Lectures	____	____	____	____	____	____
(g) County Mental Health Clinic	____	____	____	____	____	____
(h) Star Power	____	____	____	____	____	____
(i) Black Problems Session	____	____	____	____	____	____

Other:_____

_____

5. Have you heard any comments from your fellow officers about this course, its effectiveness and application to real situations?_____

_____

_____

_____

6. Was any information offered in the course redundant, that is, you already knew about it through prior education or experience?_____

_____

_____

_____

7. Should there be additional follow-up training offered in this subject matter?

Yes_____ No_____. If yes, how many hours should be used for this training?

_____.

8. When should these courses be offered: Every 6 months_____ Every year_____

other time period_____.

9. What is your overall evaluation of this course?

Very Favorable   _____
Favorable   _____
Neutral   _____
Unfavorable   _____
Very Unfavorable _____

Comments:_____

_____

_____

_____

10. One final question, would you recommend that this course be mandatory for all members of your Department? Yes_____ No_____.

With these exceptions:_____

_____

_____

Why?_____

_____

_____

THE POLICE SOCIAL
WORKER IN THEORY

THE authors have noted in each community two separate systems working on many of the same problems and with many of the same people. One defines itself as a law enforcement system, including police, courts and prisons. The front-line contact is the policeman on patrol.

The second one is the diverse social service and mental health system which provides help for many of the community's dysfunctional families. The front-line worker in much of this system is the social worker.

For most troubled people the line between the problem being expressed in terms of a law violation or a social maladjustment is artificial at best and perhaps illusionary. For the overall benefit of society, there is little point in the total separation of these two systems.

The authors strongly suggest that members of the social work profession be involved within the police system. Currently this is not common practice, but there are numerous reasons why it should be. Experience supports its practicality, even though much is yet to be documented. The authors have seen service needs and opportunities to meet them to the benefit of police, mental health professionals and people in crisis. The authors have studied other ventures which are much like their own program. These programs must be saluted as adventuresome undertakings and be encouraged to continue.

This issue will be explored within this chapter in the following manner: first, some of the problems seen within the current police service system will be examined; second, the social work profession and the problems seen for it in such an amalgamation will be discussed; third, some of the functions to be served by social workers within the police system will be suggested.

The first question undoubtedly to be asked by both police officers and social workers might be, "What business does a social worker have in police work?" Neither profession, heretofore, has recognized or accepted the extent to which police officers provide basic social services. Nor is there any recognition of the mutuality of both clients and problems faced by each.

As the authors have defined the term "police service," it is a helping role officers perform for those in emotional pain and in derranged and disorganized states. It encompasses numerous variations of crisis contact with the citizenry, plus much more ongoing involvement with the chronically dysfunctional. Examples of such cases were provided in Chapter II. It might be pertinent to again emphasize that some 80 percent of all police work is noncriminal in nature. The police officer on patrol provides most of the basic services available on weekends, and from 5:00 P.M. to 9:00 A.M., when most social agencies are closed.

Consider now a few of the problems encountered currently in the providing of police service. The following five points are noted and will be considered for brief discussion. They are as follows: lack of recognition, isolation and compartmentalization, inadequate training, information blockage, and lastly, overlap and duplication. These points are individually important but, moreover, in combination contribute to and reinforce the inadequacy of the present police service endeavor.

Lack of Recognition

Currently officers in their police service role are given little recognition either by the community or by their police system. There are no rewards or acknowlegdements for a service job well done. Officers are expected to perform adequately with limited training and in most instances with little or no support services. Statistics are not kept which might enrich our understanding of the problems encountered and which might lead to further improvement in police techniques in handling of such calls. In fact, good recording, documentation and statistical evaluation might well lead to an altered concept of the needs within the community and from there to modifications of the social service delivery system. Currently one can only say that social problems prevented or coped with by the officer on patrol are most often problems unrecognized within the community.

Isolation and Compartmentalization

In not recognizing or legitimizing its own service aspect, the police system has encouraged its further isolation from the remainder of the social service community. The social service community has little understanding of the degree of service provided within the police system. They see the police officer much as he defines himself. He is "out there preventing crime and catching criminals."

Social service organizations see little value in contact with police officers. Each is seen as doing an entirely separate, if not mutually incompatible, job within the community. The social worker might even see it as in the best interest of his client to not share information with a police officer.

The police officer on the other hand sees many of the clients of the social agencies unhelped and with social workers unavailable during the evening and night hours when so many problems express themselves. Experiencing such situations police officers often tend to become cynical and distrustful of social workers.

Such isolation results in narrowed vision and in limiting the scope of solutions that might be sought by both social service agencies and the police system working together.

Inadequate Training

Officers to date have had to learn police service through war stories and through a trial and error system. This is a costly, unproductive and generally inadequate way in which to learn. The problems dealt with in police service are too important to be left to such a casual learning process.

This is not to suggest that the techniques of the mental health profession can be transmitted straight across the board to police problem situations. They cannot. It is vital that both the police system and the mental health professionals recognize this. It is suggested that many techniques and methods of the helping professions do, with only slight modification, work well in police service.

After four years of working with police officers, the authors are conditioned at this point to state for the officer reader that they are not speaking of long-term, in-depth interviews. We refer to quick diagnostic skills and to many helping techniques that are more a matter of attitude and approach than of time.

For the social worker and the other mental health professionals, it should also be pointed out that there is much that can be learned from the police officer as well. Officers have developed many practical, well-tested techniques for working with individuals in conflict and anger. The use of their physical presence, the use of their bodies to isolate combatants from each other and many other crisis-helping techniques are worth learning and modifying for treatment use.

It is not important in the long run whether officer or social worker learns more from the other. It is important, however, that there be a more structured and formalized understanding of how to provide good police service. Officers are, in many instances, the first contact for the community's mentally ill. They play a central role in many other emotional crisis situations. Officers must be more fully trained in helping and diagnostic skills. This is necessary if they are to be effective in dealing with the behavioral and emotional disorders of their patrol areas.

Information Blockage

Police service, by operating in a vacuum, profits neither from adequate providing of information to other agencies or in receiving such from them. In not acknowledging the extent of its own service, the remainder of the community neither recognizes nor credits the extent of police involvement, labor or concern.

Officers do involve themselves in family problems. When opportunity occurs they refer such families to social agencies. On those occasions when they subsequently contact such an agency, they are usually told they should play no further role as helper.

The officer, in his district, often has much information to impart. Most would be willing to do so if dealt with openly in turn. The courtesy of a follow-up report on police referred families might well bring officers into a partnership role. Presently officers often end up as antagonists instead.

It is well to remember that an officer may have a more integrated knowledge of the district and may have been more intimately involved with its families over far more years than the social agency representative.

The police myth that officers work only on crime and the prevention of crime has been well accepted. The agency representative may suspect, therefore, that the officer is seeking social information for some ulterior motive. Information, if given under this impression, will at best be provided inadequately and grudgingly. This attitude is mutually reinforcing. Police officers in such a system share very little information in turn with social agencies.

It is to be hoped that with a greater acceptance of the police service role, and with recognition that information shared is to the benefit of families in distress, the situation can be improved.

Overlap and Duplication

Police officers do have numerous contacts in crisis situations. They also have many ongoing contacts with the chronically dysfunctional. It is in this latter area that the issue of overlap and duplication is most significant. It has been found that the chronic police-problem family is most often also one of the community's "hard core" social-problem families. Many of these families have been seen over the years by various combinations of the community's social service system. Police service is included as a part of the foregoing.

Particularly with our "hard core" client, the agency involvements are numerous and duplication extensive. It is with this group especially that consistency and follow-through are most important. Unfortunately, in most cases, there is insufficient continuity of service to accomplish the changes desired. This overlap was demonstrated most clearly in the training seminars. As a part of the seminars, police and corrections officers, public health nurses, mental health, welfare and juvenile court personnel were brought together. The initial contact was, in most instances, one of guardedness and reserve. "Who are those people and what do they have to do with our job?"

The mutuality was almost always found in terms of their frustrated efforts with the same families. Someone would, for instance, mention the Johnsons or the Fraziers, and others would nod with recognition. "And whatever happened to Mary Lou?" Or, "I remember Ron's brother. He was on my caseload when all those stolen cars were found."

For purposes of illustration community services were pictured as a large daisy. The petals were as numerous as the services a community provided. The outer portion of each of these petals represented the specialized services of an agency and those less likely of duplication. As one moves toward the center one finds overlap and duplication until, at the very center, the "hard core" family is revealed. The illustration can be carried further in pointing out that this center provides the seeds of further community social service problems.

It has come to be accepted as almost a rule of the system that the more agencies involved with any particular family, the less adequately were the services used. This certainly proved true in a rough experiential way through involvement with the police-problem family. If this says something of the lack of structure and organization of such families, it may also say something of their treatment need. It may suggest that such families should be provided a more "parenting" or supervisory type of helping relationship than is usually provided. The duplications of service were obviously both costly and inefficient.

In summary of the foregoing five points, the following may be said: Community services would be vastly improved by some cooperation and further coordination of effort; the recognition and acceptance of police service is supported; cooperation should be encouraged between the police system and the other community social service agencies; involvement and cooperation is usually mutually reinforcing. It should result in improved communication between police and social services and, therefore, in improved community service by both officer and social worker. Most police calls are only a variation on the theme of social dysfunction within the community.

The Police Social Worker

The social worker that is recommended for the police setting is a trained professional. He has completed a two-year post graduate course leading to either an MSW (Master of Social Work) or MSS (Master of Social Services) degree. To work competently within the police system, he should also have put this training into practice and to have gained enough professional identification to feel free and comfortable in working on his own.

This social worker should have developed diagnostic skills and an ability to work with and help individuals and families with social problems. Much of his interest should be in counseling, in helping people through talking to throughly explore feelings about what they have experienced. Through such talk (interviewing) people are helped to a better understanding of their own particular patterns of behavior. Such knowledge is one step toward learning to modify destructive or unproductive behavior.

The social worker should have training and experience in working with families. He will need to be capable of making a good family diagnosis by evaluating intellectual, emotional, physical and cultural resources within the family group. In doing so he will be able to make recommendations to the police system for their further action, or make appropriate referral to a social agency.

Beyond such skills as evaluating and counseling with individuals and families, social workers traditionally develop a large store of knowledge of community resources. They should know the agencies and services within a community, where to obtain legal advice, medical care, financial aid, counseling, and services for children.

Social workers work closely with the other major mental health professionals, psychiatrists and psychologists. These three operate as a team in many mental health or child guidance clinics. Social workers, with masters degree training, are in social agencies and additionally work as supportive personnel in some non-social settings, such as hospitals, courts or public health organizations. In this way social workers often form an unofficial communication network which spreads through both private and public social agencies, courts, hospitals and schools.

These foregoing social work functions are seen as valuable additions to the police system and to its service work within the community.

There are elements of risk in social worker involvement within the police system. There are risks physically, emotionally and professionally. There are risks for the police system as well but probably not as many.

It is not easy to move into another system where your fellow workers may be hostile. Some social workers may feel there is risk in the generalized nature of police service. Many social workers in their professional development desire to become more and more specialized. Many of the more skillful quickly move into supervision or administration. The police social worker, however, has to operate very much as a generalist. He must be prepared to make field evaluations and referrals, train, consult and advise.

The social worker moving into the police system will need to consider his feelings about authority. Can he work with authority? Can he use it to help others? Authority *per se* is not seen as either good or bad. The need for and use of authority is certainly one of the realities of the police system. Social workers and other mental health professionals can contribute to the best use of such authority for both the client and society.

Lastly it may be suggested that there is risk in moving out into the community, especially at night when other social services are unavailable. There is risk as well in working with an acting-out population for whom few good treatment techniques have been developed.

> There is a story of the social worker who left his office one fine day for a stroll in the park. The sun shone as he walked along a wooded path at the edge of a lake. The path turned and he suddenly saw a man off shore, in deep water and in desperate circumstances. The man struggled, floundering, going under to rise again. He spewed water and thrashed wildly.

The social worker resolutely stood and observed. The man continued to struggle. The social worker continued to watch, though with growing indications of concern. Coming up again, the man was able, with one last desperate breath, to yell, "Help!"

The social worker immediately leaped to the rescue, and succeeded in pulling the man out. He looked down at this poor man, still gasping and wretching on the bank, and said with obvious relief, "I was so worried. Thank heavens you could call for help."

There is a fairly basic question in this story. That is, must every call for help be clearly articulated? It is believed that there is a large population within the community who communicate most clearly by their actions. It is suggested that it is the responsibility of mental health professionals to recognize and interpret these actions as cries for help.

The social worker in this story at least did not stand as some professionals now seem to and ask, "And how do you feel about drowning?" For too long now all mental health professionals have backed away from police problems, considering them too dirty or too dangerous for their concern or involvement. It is time, the authors suggest, to get our feet wet again.

The concept of the police social worker is suggested by two particular social work functions. First of all, social work has traditionally been the mental health component most attuned to work out in the community. It has developed skills in working with families in their homes and in the community. Coming most recently from this tradition, it would be expected to return most easily to community work. Secondly, social work often functions as a bridging service between mental health need and various community helping systems. The obvious value in extending these activities within the police setting can easily be seen. It is time to stop defining problems in terms of social problems or police problems and redefine them as *community* problems.

In summary, there are risks in the establishment of police social worker programs. Establishing the role, and oneself in it, is a difficult and time-consuming task. It may be suggested, however, that there are broad opportunities for growth for both the professional and for the profession in such involvement.

Following is a brief statement concerning police officers trained in the authors' program. It speaks to the difficulty of working and cooperating together.

BABY, IT'S BIGGER THAN BOTH OF US!

In many years of meeting with various professionals, discussing community problems and possible solutions to them, one message has come through louder than all the rest. That message is that everyone appears to be most expert and most dogmatic in their knowledge of the other person's business. School teachers, nurses, policemen, social workers, attorneys, doctors, etc., all seem to know where the fault for the continuance of the community's problems lie. It is with the "other guy."

It can only be assumed that this tendency to blame rests in one's own frustrations. Each of us knows that he and his kind are doing their utmost to solve the problems. Why, therefore, do poverty, crime, sickness and immorality still exist in spite of all our efforts and concern?

The guilt for not having solved these problems tends to make one think in terms of blame and seek its placement elsewhere. The problem is then forgotten as one establishs why the *other* profession is at fault. It is simply a matter, then, of "them guys" just straightening up and doing their job right. And everyone knows exactly how to do the others job.

This problem, as seen by the authors, rests on frustration, narrowness and intolerance of one's own weakness. Why not accept that no one profession has all the answers? Certainly no answers will be found in fault finding between the professionals. Indeed, the problems are bigger than either social work or police work, but maybe not bigger than *both* disciplines working together. The answers, if there be any, may only be reached when we have enough self-respect and confidence in ourselves to then be tolerant of the "other guy." At that point one can again return to the issue at hand and try to establish what the individual can contribute toward a solution.

What specific contribution might social work make within the police system? Over the past four years, the authors have experienced a variety of police call situations. They would suggest the following as a partial list of police contact situations in which a social worker might contribute to better police service. In some of these the social worker can act as a direct contact person with the victim. In others he may be supportive of family members. In any situation he may well be gaining information essential to further planning and resolving of the problem.

A generalized list of such police service calls might be as follows: child abuse and neglect, incest, rape, attempted or threatened suicide, neighborhood disputes, runaway reports, psychotics, accidental death and suicide, search and rescue operations, and domestic disturbances.

In all the foregoing social work has something to contribute to both the individual in emotional pain and also to the police system. Social workers are trained and skilled interviewers. They can gather information and organize and document it in a broadly interrelated manner.

The main social work function supportive of the police system may be described under three broad headings: broker, trainer and field support.

Broker

1. Community Organization

In this capacity the social worker represents and involves the police service system with other social, mental health or medical facilities. Police needs are represented by the social worker in a middleman role. Other organizations needing an understanding of police functions and needing at times to modify and adjust to such functions are provided knowledge and interpretation.

The authors found themselves doing this constantly over the past four years, many times helping an agency understand why the police system might respond as it does. The personnel of various hospitals, clinics and institutions do not know what it is like in the policeman's world. The police officer lacks their resources and supporting services but still has to make the critical decisions. By helping such social and medical personnel to recognize the part police play in their clients' lives, they experience some client problems in a less limited context. They are in this way helped to more realistically assess the difference between client behavior within an office setting and his reported behavior in the community.

Improved social documentation would contribute to a better community understanding of police operation. Social work documentation and interpretation of police service situations would be one step in this direction.

2. Referral Planning

Referral planning is a complicated and sometimes difficult procedure. It requires an extensive knowledge of the social agency system and sometimes a personal knowledge of the personnel and philosophy of a referral institution. The social worker has his training, his knowledge of the community and developed skill in this area.

3. Information Exchange

It has often been pointed out that social workers speak their own language. Every profession has its jargon, the code words for a group of agreed upon interpretations and basic assumptions. Anyone communicates most easily with others with whom they share beliefs, assumptions, training and experience. By the use of social workers within the police system itself, a wide range of agency contacts can be opened for a needed flow of information in both directions.

PATTY

The officer was on his way out to see Patty again. He had seen her four times within the last three months. Each time it was for a different problem. Her "old man," as she described him, was in the state prison on a theft charge. Their baby girl had been removed on neglect. Patty had called this time because her apartment had been ransacked and broken up.

The social worker was asked to accompany the officer. Maybe the social worker could do something for her or with her. The officer couldn't help feeling sorry for Patty. He hoped the social worker could, in some way, help her.

Patty was a very plain looking young woman. She was attractive only in her youth and in her openness and sincerity.

She was not an intelligent person. That may have explained in part why she remained so open and honest in her talk with others.

Patty sat on a broken couch in a drab and barren room. She had packed her most precious possessions in one paper bag and had some clothes in another. Patty's most important possession was her picture album. She showed it to the social worker who had not seen either her husband or child.

Patty had open sores and bruises on both arms and legs. She had gotten these, she said, in a motorcycle accident three days ago. She needed medical care.

The social worker talked with Patty at some length. He found she had no relatives and few friends locally. What friends she did have did not sound as if they would be of much help to her. She had known them through her husband. Like him they had poor records of stability and reliability.

The social worker and the officer had opportunity to judge this more directly. Six men and three women arrived to talk with Patty. They were antagonistic rather than sympathetic. They heard that Patty had thought one of them might have taken her things. Probably because the social worker and the officer were present, nothing further developed and the group left.

The social worker checked mentally through placement or housing resources for Patty. She needed medical care soon. She would also require some financial aid and probably some good mothering or supervision. He would need to consider both some long-range plans and the immediate issue of where she might stay for tonight.

At this point, the social worker left Patty and the officer to find a public telephone. He called the agencies where Patty had been helped before. One of these, a public social agency, provided job training and supervised placement for the unskilled. The other social agency was funded by private donations and offered counseling and foster care for neglected and abused children. This agency also counseled the parents of these children.

At one of the agencies the social worker talked first to a friend he had known for several years. He checked on the social agency's policy in cases such as this and also as to the possibility of exceptions to such policy.

The social worker was given two leads by his friend, one for financial help and the other for a program providing supervised housing. The social worker also added to his store of information on Patty. Although the agency contacts with Patty had been brief, they had made some assessment of her abilities to follow through on plans made.

The one agency had helped Patty in a work placement. They knew something of her reliability, skills and work capacity. The other agency was still involved in supervising her infant in foster care. The social worker enlarged his knowledge here on Patty's relationship to both husband and child.

With a number of telephone calls the social worker sifted through the community's resources. Each call clarified possibilities in some social agency or program and often provided new leads. The social worker arranged for a nights lodging for Patty and for emergency medical care. Two days later he accompanied Patty to an agency with a program which he thought should meet her needs quite well.

This private social agency provided supervised living and job counseling. It provided what Patty needed even more, a very protective nurturing atmosphere. With this arranged the social worker ceased his planning for Patty.

This story is illustrative of the broker concept of the police social worker. The social worker functioned as a go-between for client, police system and agency. Through knowledge of resources, contacts and information sharing, Patty was helped.

Trainer

1. Skill Reinforcement

As a part of any training system, some theoretical knowledge may be supplied over short periods, such as seminar training, lectures, films, articles, etc. In the long range, however, much of what one learns is established through repeated performance and application. It is in this manner that a social worker's continued involvement in police service cases can be viewed as a training role. The social worker, in performing his job, would be demonstrating and teaching his professional skills to the police officers with whom he works. It is not recommended that social workers supplant officers within police service. It is suggested, however, that social workers provide a supportive service, bringing in their own professional skills and expertise when needed. In time, by so doing, they will contribute to a more proficient police handling of police service problems.

2. Consultation

Consultation is also a part of the more generalized trainer role. Consultation is a debriefing and discussing of what another professional has done within a given set of circumstances. It provides other professionals, in this case the police officer, a chance to consider alternatives, in a sense to play Monday quarterback to the Saturday game. Considering options, good procedures can be reinforced, while weak ones can be discussed and new options suggested.

STEVEN

It was a Sunday afternoon. The social worker was called at home by an officer from the department's juvenile section. One of the patrolmen had called in with some questions about a five-year-old boy. The boy's name was Steven. The patrolman had thought it might be a matter of either neglect or abuse.

As the social worker and the officer rode out, they discussed what little information they had. On three separate occasions neighbors had lodged complaints with the police department. Steven had killed a puppy by beating it with a stick. Steven had released the brake on his father's car. The car had rolled out and across the street breaking through a neighbor's fence. Steven was seen at 5:30 A.M. collecting all the neighbor's newspapers. The patrolman, in talking to Steven's mother about this last incident, thought she was extremely angry and punishing.

The social worker told his companion that he would be considering several possibilities. He would be looking for the adequacy of parental care and supervision. Maybe these parents didn't care. Possibly they let their children run loose to do whatever they might within the neighborhood. If so they would see signs of indifference and neglect, perhaps in the physical care or perhaps in attitude and interest.

The incidents reported might also suggest the possibility of an emotionally disturbed child. They would look for other signs of disturbed or abnormal behavior. Did he have any playmates? Were there signs of uncontrolled rages? Was he a withdrawn, uncommunicative child? Was Steven responding to stress within the family?

A third possibility that came quickly to mind was hyperactivity. Steven might present a pattern of oversensitivity to all stimuli. They would check on his attention span. Were there signs of uncoordination or other indications of organicity? Maybe mother's anger resulted only from the strain and frustration of having to cope with such an active child.

The social worker and the officer arrived at the house. The officer was interested in testing his own perceptions of this child. Steven's mother was upset by the further police contact but was willing to talk about Steven.

Little by little the picture emerged. The officer watched as the social worker knelt down to talk with Steven. The social worker talked with him mostly about his toys and games. They watched Steven play. In observing Steven and in talking with mother, a picture of hyperactivity became clearer.

Steven was developing behavior problems as well. Other children found him difficult to play with. The puppy had not liked the way Steven played and had bitten him. Steven had attempted to punish the puppy and had overdone it. He often woke up early in the morning. He had watched the newsboy come by on his bicycle, envied him and decided on that morning to play newsboy himself.

There were no signs of neglect or abuse. The social worker, however, did talk with this mother about services of a family guidance clinic. Counseling and in some instances medication were thought to help. In any case Steven should be worked with now. His first years at school would put him under additional pressure.

On the trip home the social worker and the officer reviewed the experience. The social worker elaborated further on what he had seen and checked with the officer as to his observations.

The story of Steven points up the social worker's trainer role. In this situation he transmitted knowledge to the officer through demonstration and discussion. The officer might, on some other occasion, telephone the social worker for consultation only. In this way the officer can check his perception against that of the social worker, knowing better what to present and what to ask of the social worker from this earlier training.

Field Support

1. Field Evaluation

There are many situations where an officer might use a professional assessment of the psychological or social dynamics of a case. Police involvement with psychotic individuals, neglect or abuse situations, or any of a number of other "service" calls would be enhanced through social work skills. Good field evaluations would lead to earlier and more appropriate decisions at these points of crisis.

There are no perfect decisions. There are no all-inclusive solutions. In some instances hospitalization might not be best for the mentally disturbed individual. Placement in institutional or foster care is not always the best plan for the child.

Whatever the decision the officers subsequent report to either hospital or court could be reinforced by additional information. The social worker, as an outside professional, would add one more perspective to these ambiguous situations that officers encounter daily.

2. Crisis Counseling

Somewhere beyond the area of conflict management and crisis resolution lies further counseling need. It is acknowledged, of course, that there are situations where only the "referree" may be required. There are others, however, in which further exploration is a necessity. In these the social worker can be introduced, with the officer going on about his business. This could be viewed as a transfer by the officer of his service case. The case may have moved beyond the officer's degree of capability or outside his area of felt responsibility. Many crisis situations require further social planning and arrangements for community support. In accidental death or suicide, for example, other family members or friends may need to be contacted. Arrangements occasionally involve seeking someone to come in and stay with the grieving parties. A variety of time consuming activities may take place as a part of crisis containment and support.

3. Short-term Counseling and Referral Interviewing

There are police service cases that can be helped by short-term counseling. This means a maximum of five or six follow-up contacts focused on problem clarification and an assessment of the community's referral resources. The object is to direct those who can profit from such help into the appropriate helping service. In this way some seemingly chronic police service cases can and have been shifted from the police caseload. Successful referral is, of course, far more complicated than providing a person with an agency name and address. It entails understanding the views of the person as to his particular problem and, further, if and to what degree he is motivated to change. The police social worker is not seen as a professional who provides long-term therapy. His use is held to the immediate, and his focus is always short-term.

BONNIE JAMES

It was evening. The social worker was called and asked to meet the officer at a family home. He was told it was an incest situation. Bonnie, the sixteen-year-old daughter, had reported her father at the juvenile court.

Two officers had gone out to talk with the family. The father panicked. He was now locked in the bathroom crying. There was some fear that this man might kill himself.

An officer introduced the social worker to Mrs. James. She had very little to say. Mrs. James was obviously hurt by what had happened. She was also angry. Mrs. James was concerned about her husband. She feared he might be arrested and lose his job.

The social worker talked for awhile with Mr. James through the bathroom door. He then came out, sat down and talked with the social worker and the two officers. He continued to cry. While doing so he sat slumped in the chair shading his eyes with his hand.

Mr. James, too, was fearful that he would go to prison. A number of years ago he had stolen from an employer. He had been placed on probation. This probation period was just now ending.

The officers explained the law to Mr. James and what information they would need for their report. Mr. James did admit his guilt. He claimed it had only happened once, though.

Both parents made complaints about Bonnie: She wouldn't mind; she always wanted to run around and wouldn't come home when she was supposed to.

The social worker talked with Mr. James, evaluating in two areas. First, was Mr. James upset enough to commit suicide? If he were, they might need to take him into custody. Second, what recommendations might he eventually be making to the court? Should this man be in prison? Should he be separated from this family now for the well-being of the other children?

The two officers and the social worker held a brief conference. They decided to leave Mr. James in his home for the present. The signs for suicidal potential were weak. He was not seen as likely to molest any of the other children. Plans were made with the family for follow-up contacts by the social worker and by the officers. The social worker was asked to complete a social summary report to be attached to the officers' report.

The next morning the social worker telephoned the social worker at the juvenile court. He checked for her impressions of Bonnie and for further information on the incest. That afternoon he returned to the James' home and talked with Mr. and Mrs. James further.

A series of interviews were set up to explore the situation. From these interviews information would be developed to help both police and the courts in whatever decision they might reach.

The social worker learned that the sexual relationship between Mr. James and Bonnie covered a period of years. It was, in many ways, a long-term affair. Bonnie and her father had even double dated with Bonnie's high school friends on one occasion. As this all came out, Mrs. James became much more openly angry at both Mr. James and Bonnie.

Mr. James was convicted but not sent to prison. He was again placed on probation. The court thought it to society's advantage to have Mr. James remain employed and in the family. Bonnie remained in foster care, with Mr. James paying the cost of this as well.

It was recognized that there were continuing and serious problems within this family. Arrangements were made with a public mental health agency to provide counseling. Mr. and Mrs. James were seen weekly, and eventually Bonnie joined them in these counseling sessions.

In this case of Bonnie and her parents, there is an example of crisis counseling, field evaluation and short-term referral planning. The need for such service is present in many police calls. This may well be true of criminal cases, as well as those more clearly defined as police service calls.

Summary

Police service is seen as an important and vital part of the police system. A need to improve and upgrade the officer's techniques and procedures within police service is also acknowledged. Many problems within both the police system and the community as to the recognition and acceptance of police service have been noted. Until this is achieved police service will remain the ragged stepchild of police activity.

The authors feel that there are advantages to social work, the police system and to the citizen in a joining of police and social work efforts. Social work would again, in this setting, function in a deeply involved way within the community. An opportunity is available for police social work to pioneer in further understanding of the "acting-out" client. Involvement with the police system provides insights into new problem areas. It provides opportunity to experiment with the use of different professional techniques in handling the great varities of police crisis contacts.

For the police officer there is professional support and the opportunity to learn from another's areas of competency. There is, for the police system, the possibility for improved communication and for informational sharing with the remainder of the community's service systems. Social work counseling and referral should relieve some of the pressure to police service. For the citizen there would be better and quicker field evaluation of problems and a more proficient handling of the human interactions of service cases.

The authors, therefore, strongly recommend that the police system seek, and that social workers offer to become, community brokers, trainers and supporters working on police service problems. As has been previously states, "Baby, it's bigger than both of us."

Questions for Discussion

1. What do the authors view as skills that social workers might bring to police service?
2. In what types of police calls might social workers support a police officer?
3. How do the authors see social work involvement as improving police and community information exchange?
4. What are the possible risks for the police system or for social service agencies in the use of police social workers?
5. What five points are presented as inhibitory to good police service?
6. Why do the authors suggest the community might be better helped with more cooperation between police and social service agencies?
7. In what ways might a police social worker be of use to a police officer or to the police agency?
8. In what ways might a social worker help in a domestic disturbance call, incest or with a psychotic?

Chapter V

THE POLICE SOCIAL
WORKER IN PRACTICE

THE authors' awareness of the need for a police social worker came through direct patrol experience and discussion with police officers. Officers told of their great frustration in working with a variety of human problems. Many were concerned about their own inadequate training. They saw much of what they did as outside their basic area of responsibility and personal interest. Officers were particularly annoyed at the lack of resource and backup for social problems encountered on nights and weekends.

Social Work Students

In the Spring of 1971, after one year's experience with police, the authors approached the county sheriff's department and the local graduate school of social work with a unique proposal. The authors would supervise social work students in field training if their placements were in patrol cars with deputies. Both the sheriff and the school were willing to consider this.

The aim of the program was two-fold: to take back to the social service community, through the training of its newest members, knowledge of the social problems confronting the police officer on patrol; on the other hand the authors wished to demonstrate to the police system that there was a contribution to be made by social workers in working with police problem families. These were the goals set in developing this experimental program.

One of the first issues of concern was that of safety. Both police officers and social workers were apprehensive. Would such a program place either or both of the parties at risk? Officers were afraid that they might have to protect these "helpers" at greater risk to themselves. The social workers' misjudgements or very presence might encourage adverse citizen reaction. Social workers, on the other hand, expressed concern that police might callously mishandle sensitive situations and thereby encourage physical confrontation. In spite of educational efforts, each remained inadequately informed about the other. Police officers apparently could not believe that social workers ever confronted anger or violence, or that they walked the fine line of its potential. Social workers did not realize the extent to which the average police officer had learned to talk his way through and around violence.

The authors met with the officers at evening role call to discuss the selection of the students who would ride. It was established clearly that they would have to be male, experienced if possible, with mature and calm demeanors. The records of the potential students were reviewed with this in mind and discussed with the lieutenant in charge at the point of final selection.

At the request of the sheriff, the project did provide insurance coverage for these students. Periods of mutual training were also arranged so that both officer and "student" could explore and hopefully resolve some of their mutual concerns. The students met in a group with the authors for three hours weekly, and the involved deputies were encouraged to attend also. One of the authors also met with each student individually, usually on a weekly basis.

Another factor which helped to make the initial program possible had to do with the authors' familiarity to both police and graduate school. Having dealt with both before, each had some knowledge of what could or could not be done. It was also very much to our advantage that the social work school needed field placements that year.

For this initial year, three first-year male students were assigned. Their ages were twenty-four, twenty-eight and thirty-seven. They were selected and supervised by the social work member of the project. He reviewed their school applications and looked for qualities or maturity, common sense and stability. Two expressed some interest in or had some experience in the correctional area. The lieutenant who was both the department liaison officer and the commander of the swing shift selected three volunteer deputies. Thus the teams were established. A team would hopefully work together one night a week for nine months, the duration of the school year. Three nights of the week would thus be covered. Another half-day a week of each student's time was involved in counseling and follow-up work with clients.

Each team was to work within a district, patrolling generally within the evening hours of 5:00 P.M. to midnight. It was hoped that they could often function as a "wild car," the team providing backup and support over several districts. It was anticipated that the team would respond particularly to those calls requiring counseling and other social services.

Since there was still much initial apprehension about and within the teams, our first direction to the students was that they *observe*. This was agreed to but quickly abandoned. Students were involved in "doing" long before the authors had anticipated their being so. This, it is believed, developed from the apprehension of both student and officer. Team members wished to test out quickly whether the concept was feasible for them or not. If not they wanted to know immediately.

It was found that students were coming back very shortly demanding more preparation with statements such as, "You haven't taught me how to work with a potential suicide yet."

Upon further questioning this student described his activities of the previous evening. "The young man sat in a car with a loaded revolver pointed at his head, threatening to kill himself."

The student was handed a hand-pack radio and sent in to discuss with this young man whether he really did wish to complete the act or not. The potential suicide, angry and hurt over a broken love affair, decided he would much rather talk about it than take his own life. Letting the officer have the gun, he then sat down with the student social worker to unload much of his anger outwardly and verbally, rather than to punish the lady by his death.

This example and numerous others were seen as quick testing of the team concept. Could a social worker be an asset rather than merely company or liability? Was the officer put at further risk? Would these individuals handle situations in any way differently than an officer might have?

All of these questions were eventually resolved in a manner

supportive of these two professions cooperatively solving patrol problems together. The students were exposed to situations involving death, physical confrontation and some high drama. They handled themselves well and were seen as an asset to the department.

Much of the contribution, however, came in more mundane situations. They were able to help greatly in the referral process, provided knowledge of community resources, and aided in follow-up planning with chronic problem cases. In these areas they added a dimension to police service that had not been present previously. This social work activity complimented and rounded out the officers crisis intervention and conflict resolution activity.

Many of the cases, however, were merely variations of what the student social worker could expect in his later professional life. The students did carry back to their peers information about the types of problems worked with by police service. Other students were excited and intrigued by the possibility of work with these kinds of clients. Through this some professionals within the community gained their initial awareness of police service.

The following is part of a report from three social work students for the school year 1971-1972. It is taken from their final evaluation of the year's field placement.

> Two other observations consequently came to our attention while "riding along" each week. First of all, we were all impressed by the lack of community resources for meeting emergency crises. The county hospital crisis unit was the only resource available on a twenty-four hour basis. And this resource could be used only for those mental cases where possible "injury to self or others" was indicated. There was no resource for the myriad other crises needing immediate attention. We all feel this problem needs urgent attention.
>
> Secondly, we discovered that community agencies were not meeting the needs of the vast number of people even during the eight hours a day their doors were open. One needs only to ride along with the police for one or two days to meet person after person who has never heard of the mental health clinic, young drug user or alcoholic treatment center. Although we did not take an accurate survey, we feel it is safe to say that at least half of the people we saw had not made use of any mental health

agency. It may be that the social service agencies are failing to
reach those who need their help the most, the ones police deal
with day in and day out.

It is felt that the impressions of the students were accurate. It
corroborates much of what the authors experienced as well. Numerous social problems have been seen with a far too limited access
to social resources. This is, in fact, what led the authors to seek the
placement of students within a police setting. Such placements
might serve as a vehicle for better education of the social service
community. Through them it is hoped that some awareness of the
many problems currently outside social agency systems will be
provided.

The student social work-police officer teams were successful. It
was demonstrated to both social worker and officer that they
could be effective in the field. They were neither a hindrance nor a
danger to the officer. They also greatly widened the options of
help available to police service problems. Because of this initial
success the authors were able to continue with two more years of
student field placements. During the second year a woman student was placed with the program. She worked within the juvenile section.

A field placement within a police setting is extremely challenging to the student. Learning occurs but in a more unplanned,
unscheduled manner than might happen through more traditional settings.

There were obvious identity problems for the social work student. As he was learning who and what he was professionally, he
was at the same time being challenged by both officer and client as
to what his function could and should be. This combines quite
often to be both personally threatening and growth producing. In
all instances, fortunately, the latter did occur. No student was
totally overwhelmed by the experience. At times, however, bore-
dom was a problem, since during some evenings little seemed to
be going on.

Commenting on three years of student placements within the
department, officers have made the following observations. Having the social worker present, they suggested, often diminished
rather than heightened citizen-officer confrontation. Officers

could describe particular calls in which they clearly anticipated challenge and harassment, and credited the presence of the social worker with it not occurring. The public, in such instances, saw the social workers' presence as defining police intervention differently, in a more helping way. And they, therefore, responded in an altered manner. This pleased the officers, who disliked being manipulated into confrontation.

Officers also became aware of a number of police service contacts that did not require continued police presence. On some occasions, after the initial contact, the social worker could be left to complete his task while the officer continued on to another call. Typical services included quick diagnostic evaluations for the mentally ill, crisis counseling for domestic disturbance cases, and help in runaway and incest situations. These students also provided the link between police service and other community social services. In follow-up activities they searched for appropriate resources for children in need and tried to resolve other chronic problem situations about which the officer was concerned but did not have time to pursue.

Let us at this point digress to describe two cases that in some part illustrate the complexity of problems existing in the community. Both cases occurred during one student's evening "ride-a-long."

THE SMITHS

The first call came in the late afternoon and involved continued but petty thievery. Mr. and Mrs. Smith claimed that things were being taken from their home whenever they left the house to shop or accomplish any task. They were quite sure their nearby neighbors were guilty. These neighbors were two ex-convicts from out of state, and Mr. Smith believed they took things from their house as the easiest way to support themselves. Mr. Smith informed the team that there was a teenage girl, the daughter of a local ex-convict, also living with these men. He thought some of his household items were probably being sold to provide all of them with drugs.

Mr. Smith, a marginal worker, possibly retarded and certainly poorly educated, expressed great anger and frustration with his situation. His wife, stocky, short and barefooted, was obviously the more intelligent of the two. She carefully helped her husband to explain, while at the same time providing some supervision for the five small children running around the yard.

The shack in which the Smiths lived was inadequate in both construction and housekeeping standards. The Smiths seemed satisfied with it, however. Mrs. Smith told the team that she had been raised barefoot herself in a rural area as one of nine children. She was obviously repeating the pattern of this raising with very little discomfort.

Mrs. Smith, too, was quite angry about the thievery. Food was stolen, and this meant that often she and the children went without. Mrs. Smith raised one additional point of concern, that of their own broken sewer line which emptied out into the back yard. Her children, barefoot as she, played around and through it, and she had been told it was probably unsanitary and unhealthy.

The team was, therefore, provided with a fairly complete list of social problems. One can think in terms of the intellectual, educational or cultural standards of the family. They were financially limited and with more children than they could adequately feed, clothe and supervise. Were the neighbors really stealing from these people who had so little themselves? Without any apparent proof, how could they approach the men next door?

The problems of the sewer and sanitation were additional concerns. Mrs. Smith described her attempts to involve public health department personnel. She had received a variety of answers as to where departmental responsibility lay and as to which agency she might talk to further. In the final analysis, nothing had changed.

The Smiths were asked about the owner of the house they were renting, thinking that he perhaps could be encouraged to maintain the property more adequately. The officer and social worker were given a name which they recognized as one of the city's liberal professional men. This was a man well known within the community for his supposed great concerns for mankind. In talking to him later, the student discovered that his interest in mankind did not extend to his individual tenants. Here was both a sobering and disillusioning experience.

The officer and the student both felt overwhelmed as they

tried to decide where to start in helping the Smiths.

* * * *

THE TAYLORS

The team had barely left this situation when they were informed of a breaking and entry in progress. They pulled up at the small house on the break-in report just as two other cars arrived as well. The house was set well back from the road, one of the main thoroughofares between two large shopping centers. The house was small and modest and looked as if it had been originally constructed as a summer cottage.

A man in his forties, Mr. Taylor, told the officers and the student that they should be looking for two teenage girls. Mr. Taylor said he had returned home earlier that afternoon from a long trip. He had been accompanied by his small son, and both of them had then taken a nap. There had been a knocking on the front door in the early evening, and by the time he became aware enough to answer it, he heard chipping and prying at the side door. He had at that point telephoned the police.

Mr. Taylor said he had been very quiet as he peered through a side window and observed the two teenage girls trying to break in. He was quite sure he could identify them easily. They had run off as he was talking to the police.

Some of the officers spread out quickly and began searching. Shortly thereafter they found the two girls in the brush. They were working their way up the highway to an old car which seemed to have been abandoned there. The officers had already noted this car and checked by radio for registration. The car was reported to have been stolen. The two girls were brought back to the front yard and positively identified by Mr. Taylor.

The girls were ages eighteen and sixteen and said that they were sisters. In their purses were a variety of tools, including screwdrivers, heavy knives and pliers. There had been an attempt to disguise themselves in part by one wearing the other girl's glasses and having quickly put her hair up under a bandanna. Neither were overtly concerned about the arrest. It seemed they had anticipated the possibility, and neither was willing to provide more than the basic facts of identification to the officers.

The student social worker present wondered to himself about the help either of these girls might receive in being put through the system. How much cooperation could one expect from the parents of these girls? He began to ask himself about the possibility of other members within the family also being in trouble or at least preparing for it.

While waiting around for the officers to complete their investigation by checking for latent prints and other evidence, the social worker was approached by Mr. Taylor. He seemed at loose ends, and apparently wanted to talk to someone during this interim. He began by mentioning how frightened his three-year-old boy was of the police officers. He said little Johnny was still hiding in the house, and that he had only peered out from behind the curtains once to see what the officers were doing. He then explained that other officers had been out just a week or two previously to serve papers on him, these having something to do with the custody of his son.

With little further encouragement Mr. Taylor began to explain. He had remarried, for the second time, to a much younger woman some five years ago. About a year and a half ago his teenage son from the previous marriage appeared and asked to move in with them. His wife, Susan, said that it would not work out well. The house was so small. But she had finally agreed at his insistence.

Mr. Taylor then told the student in a quite manner-of-fact way how his son then became sexually involved with his "stepmother." With his wife again pregnant, Mr. Taylor discovered the involvement, and there was a period of hurt and anger within the family. It was resolved with his son taking Susan and moving off to a house about half a mile down the road. His grandchild had been born and Mr. Taylor was in the process of a divorce. He had recently removed his three-year-old son, bringing Johnny back to live with him. He insisted that Johnny's living with his half-brother as stepfather was not at all proper. The mother was, at this time, attempting to regain custody of the child.

Any discussion of these two cases must be prefaced with the clearly noted fact that no member of either of these families had requested counseling-type help. It was further assumed that neither the burglars nor the attempted burglars in either of these two calls would be likely to seek this type of help.

In both the Smith and the Taylor cases, however, there were individuals with clear needs for guidance and counseling, either for their benefit or that of society. No one was under any illusion that what was being done currently would change the situations much. The calls were in many ways typical and frustrating. The problems were complex and involved, and they were probably representative of long-standing social dysfunction. These calls certainly can be defined in terms of both crime and social problem issues.

Solutions for problems such as the foregoing are often presented in terms of extremes. Some will talk of society's failures in its permissive approaches. At the other extreme may be those who advocate punishment and strict social controls. For some time the common view has assigned these two simplistic approaches to the police and social work professions now being discussed. Policemen are tough, hard-headed, brutal and unfeeling. Social workers are soft, kind, muddle-headed and sensitive. Like all stereotypes these are convenient but misleading. Both systems, police and mental health, are closer to agreement than they often understand.

Hiring a Police Social Worker

In the spring of 1972, the authors were contacted by the county sheriff with a proposal. He asked that the authors cooperate in planning with their personnel division for the hiring of a social worker and a social work aide to work full time within the police system. This proposal was based upon the department's comfort with that first year's social work-officer teams. The accomplishments of those three teams that year led the department to consider expansion. Certain public monies were then available, and it was the view of the department that they could be used advantageously in this manner. The authors, therefore, sat down with the personnel division to work out the proposed standards and job descriptions for such a social worker and an aide.

The funds to be used did not materialize. Based upon this interest, however, the project sought and obtained the money to hire a social worker. He was to be employed to work with police officers on patrol in a support capacity. In conjunction with the sheriff's department, a number of applicants were screened. The standards for such an employee, and the general areas in which they saw him functioning were again explored with the deputies. At their request the deputies were included in the screening process. Applicants were requested to ride on patrol as part of their application procedure. Deputies were, in this way, accorded the right to evaluate and recommend toward the selection. This also provided the applicants with an opportunity to consider the realities of the job more adequately.

All applicants were cleared and screened much as the department did for its own hiring of officers. The criterion was a person with a masters degree in social work, a declared interest or experience in law enforcement or corrections, an inclination to work in crisis counseling, a personality that could adjust to the varied demands of the job and, lastly, a willingness to work during swing-shift hours. The job clearly required investment and a willingness to pioneer and risk. The job was at best ambiguous and undefined.

Training continued to be the primary activity of the project. The hiring of a social worker was seen as the establishment of a year-round, permanent service component. The student social work placement would continue as well during the school year. The police social worker would, it was felt, reinforce by his continued field experience the ability to teach relevant material to the classes. In this sense the teaching and service components of the project would be mutually compatible and supportive of each other. Through training the officers knew better how to evaluate and handle emotional crisis situations and how to more effectively employ the police social worker in their behalf. The police social worker for his part could keep the authors more aware of ongoing problems and training needs for the department.

A young man with the established qualifications was hired. He began his work in the early summer of 1972. This police social worker received his professional supervision, his salary and his overall task assignments from the project. His day-to-day work within the department was supervised by the liaison lieutenant who commanded the swing shift on which he worked. This arrangement was administratively awkward but was the best that could be done. Given the understanding and the good personal relationship between the liaison lieutenant and the project director, this proved to be a workable arrangement.

Following the intial orientation and training, the police social worker was assigned a three-fold task: to gather information on social problems as experienced by patrol officers; to evaluate these in terms of the social service system; and to establish the parameters within which a professional social worker might function in this police system.

The police social worker position can best be described through some case examples from his practice.

MARITAL PROBLEM

The social worker was called at night and asked to stop by the hospital. Mrs. Rollin had been beaten by her husband. The officer did not want to take a complaint. In his experience this seldom accomplished much. This case sounded very much like others in which nothing came of such action.

The social worker met Mrs. Rollin. She was extremely attractive. Mrs. Rollin also had a way of encouraging mens' interest in her. The social worker found himself feeling protective and concerned about her.

The next day the social worker telephoned and arranged to meet with the Rollins at their home. Mrs. Rollin had returned home from the hospital that morning. She introduced the social worker to her husband. Mr. Rollin was embarrassed. He admitted having hit his wife before. He had often called her a "whore" and accused her of being an "unfit mother."

This was an extremely disturbed home. There were constant fights. While not obviously neglected, the children were not receiving the kind of parenting they should. Mr. Rollin presented himself as very concerned about the children. Both parents had been married before. Living with them were children from both of their prior marriages plus one child from this marriage.

The social worker saw the Rollins for a few counseling sessions. He maintained continuing contact by telephone and by stopping by for short interviews when problems arose.

The pattern emerged of a woman who constantly sought attention from men. Her dress, her mannerisms and her appearance radiated sex. She would then profess great innocence and shock at the attention given.

Mrs. Rollin would turn to her husband with the story of the attempted verbal or physical intimacies. Mr. Rollin felt called upon to defend his wife's virtue. He found himself both flattered and frustrated because all of these men desired *his* wife. Some of these men, however, were bigger and meaner than he.

Both parties derived certain satisfactions from this routine. The idea of Mrs. Rollin's innocence in her seductiveness permitted each to take some pleasure in their problem. There were occasions when this fantasy wore thin. It was at those times Mr. Rollin turned against his wife and beat her.

Over a two-month period the social worker continued contact. When necessary he made himself available to discuss and resolve the major disputes. With such help the family did function better.

Mrs. Rollin got a job in a supermarket stocking shelves. She said that for the first time she was given attention for what she could do and not just for being physically attractive. The rewards of this were apparently not enough, however. Mrs. Rollin did find excuses to go to work braless and provoke further male interest. Mr. Rollin was upset.

Through encouragement on the part of the social worker, the Rollins became involved in long-term therapy. The social worker contacted a number of agencies. A nearby medical facility agreed to take the family as a training case for one of the residents. The family continued to work on its problems and some further improvement was achieved. At this time the police are not being called in to resolve fights between Mr. Rollin and his wife or with the interested males.

* * * *

MUTUAL SUICIDE ATTEMPT

The police were called when a young married couple made a suicide attempt. This couple, the Allens, lived with Mr. Allen's older married sister. The officer thought that while the suicide attempt on the part of each was made to gain attention, the results could have been fatal. He contacted the social worker and asked him to meet with them at the house the day after the attempt.

The Allens were glad not to be in deeper trouble with the law and readily agreed to meet with the social worker for counseling. They met at his office once a week for five weeks.

Mr. and Mrs. Allen were young and immature. They came from a small roadside community up river. They moved to the city some four months before.

Mr. Allen had finished high school and gone into the army. He performed well there receiving both a promotion and a commendation from his commander. Mr. Allen thought he had thereby proven something to himself. At home he had never felt capable. As a boy at home his father had often downgraded him. Upon returning home the old feelings returned.

Mrs. Allen had never felt wanted or needed in her family. She did not do well in school. She was not particularly attractive. She desperately wanted to be important to someone, to belong to someone. She had known Mr. Allen in high school. He was two grades ahead of her.

When he came back from the army, she had a friend arrange a date. Mr. Allen responded to her interest. Here was a person who needed him. Her dependency made him feel important. They ran off together and got married. No one cared.

The Allens moved to the city. They found jobs in a nursing home. She washed and folded laundry and he did janitorial work. They lived in a small back room at his sister's house. Neither of them were very happy.

In order to get attention from each other, each would manufacture issues. She would propose trying to get a job as a model. He would be angry at the idea of her showing herself off. He would let her know that girls working at the nursing home wrote him notes. She would become jealous and possessive.

During one such fight he returned home to announce he had taken an overdose of some medication. He was surprised and angered to learn that she had just done the same thing.

He rushed off in the car thinking that he might run it off the road into the river. He became worried about her, turned around and drove back home. She had become frightened when he left and called the police. Both were taken to the hospital.

The Allens were very open to counseling by the social worker.

They used his guidance and direction to initiate some changes in their life. The social worker provided the support and encouragement of a good parent. They found an apartment of their own. They found some activities that both could share in. This helped them to be a little less demanding of each other.

* * * *

DOMESTIC DISTURBANCE

The couple were in their fifties. They had called the officers at least six times in the last two years. They asked help in protecting themselves from their nineteen-year-old son. The Hubbards claimed that their son, Robert, would attack them without provocation.

The officers were unable to clarify this at the times called. Robert was never present, having, as the parents explained, run off into the woods behind the house. The Hubbards had been advised to lock their son out if they did not wish him living there. They did so. Robert would then break in and return to his room in the basement.

Twice Mr. Hubbard was hospitalized with injuries inflicted by Robert. Once Mrs. Hubbard needed hospital care following a fight with Robert. On that occasion the officers had searched the basement with drawn guns. They were assured that Robert was violent and extremely dangerous.

The social worker was asked to contact the Hubbards and straighten out this problem with Robert. Twice when the social worker came to the house, Robert ran.

Some things did become clearer about the Hubbards, however. Both Mr. and Mrs. Hubbard took some pride in their difficulties. They gave numerous reasons why these problems could not be solved. They were helpless. Robert could always break in no matter how they barricaded against him. Robert had eyes like a cat. This was proven to them when they had gone out at night with flashlights to look for him in the woods. He had seen them coming.

On his third visit the social worker met Robert. Robert was big, much bigger than either of his parents. Robert was also retarded. He was fearful and did not know how he would live outside the family home. He hit them because he thought they were trying to do something to him. He would be pushed out of his room and die. They no longer loved him and he was angry.

Through further work with Robert and his parents, arrangements were made for Robert to move from home. Robert moved into a shelter home where, with guidance, he might learn to live more independently.

* * * *

NEIGHBORHOOD PROBLEM

For a year and a half the police had complaints from a nearby farming neighborhood. One family, the Barrys, had lived in this area for many years. They had been known as difficult people with whom to get along. They were clannish. The children had few friends at school.

The neighbors had handled any trouble by avoiding the Barrys. Up to now this had been possible. Within the last few years, however, the area had been subdivided. Houses were being built bringing all residents closer together physically.

Two years ago the problems increased in number and in seriousness. A year and a half ago the police were called in. Over a period of time the police received reports of horses being poisoned, a dog being shot, fences being cut, prowling and threats of injury. On one occasion an officer had to physically restrain a neighbor woman in an attack on Mr. Barry. Most of the trouble was between the Barrys and their nearest neighbors, the Richards.

The district officer became concerned that someone might be seriously hurt and asked the social worker to intervene. The social worker talked with the Barrys, the Richards and the other neighbors involved. Mr. Barry told the social worker he had moved to this area twenty-five years ago. Little by little houses crept closer and the family had to guard itself more. Two years ago the Richards had come. Certain things had happened, and he knew the Richards were behind them.

Mr. Barry was paranoid. His family shared this with him. The Richards lived a quarter of a mile away. This was within Mr. Barry's range of "critical distance," (the distance within which certain animals will feel endangered and resort to fight or flight). The Barrys were uneasy with such close neighbors, felt threatened and interpreted some possibly friendly overtures as attacks.

The Richards, in turn, became fearful and guarded. They sought out allies among the other neighbors. They had found such allies and the trouble escalated.

The social worker found that most of the neighbors had chosen sides. Some of the older established families sided with the Barrys against the newcomers. The majority of those involved sided with the Richards.

Using the local grade school principal as a go-between, the social worker eventually worked out an arrangement for all parties to meet together. Two long meetings were held at the school. Interested neighbors, police officers, a minister, the principal, the social worker and the Barry and Richards families attended. Through some bargaining, agreements for use of a common road were worked out. The Richards and the Barrys would go to town by different routes. They did not have to drive by one another's houses.

Other neighbors also became interested in how to avoid further problems within the community. None of these solutions were totally satisfying to anyone concerned, but they did start a trend. Gradually things became quieter. Mr. Barry felt less threatened. The Richards learned to fit into the neighborhood more comfortably.

* * * *

COMMUNITY NUISANCE

One of the district officers contacted the social worker about a lady in her sixties. She lived in a large, old white cadillac and often spent the evening parked somewhere in his patrol district. He worried about her health and safety. He was afraid something might happen to her sleeping out in that car at night.

During the day the lady, Miss Meyers, would park her car beside one of the city's main throughofares. There she would sit, behind the wheel, looking as if she were out for a drive. She would often stay there for most of the day with traffic moving past. In the early evening she would drive off to a nearby residential area to park and spend the night.

Miss Meyers had been well educated in her youth. She had attended two prestigious eastern women's colleges. She had two degrees, spoke five foreign languages fluently and had a mission in life: to protect the country from its enemies.

Her elaborate delusions involved the mayor and the city council. She collected evidence about an elaborate plot on their part to overthrow the federal government. The new capital of the United States was being planned for this city. The FBI received numerous letters from her concerning this plot.

Miss Meyers' harrassment brought requests from city officials to do something about this woman. This, in turn, reinforced Miss Meyers' paranoia. She was even more convinced of their viciousness and need to have her out of the way. Only she stood between them and the destruction of legitimate rule.

On one occasion there had been a court hearing. Miss Meyers had held herself together well enough throughout the hearing to keep from being committed to the state hospital. At this time the city officials had found they must and probably could live with Miss Meyers constant activity. She continued to write her letters, hand out her pamphlets and, on occasion, to picket city hall.

The social worker contacted Miss Meyers and talked with her. He found she was supported partly on welfare and partly through help from her son. The social worker contacted the welfare worker and the son. Through further planning the son arranged to come to the city to try to make some arrangements for his mother's care.

A specialized nursing home for the elderly eventually accepted Miss Meyers. She moved her possessions from the car to a room and has remained there with some satisfaction to all concerned. Miss Meyers is currently writing a book about the coming revolution and has had little time to devote to local government.

The foregoing are brief examples of cases in which the police social worker was involved. They do not illustrate the degree of anger and violence present in some police calls. The police social worker often found himself involved in these calls too. Much of what he had to work with was offensive, frustrating or depressing.

Like the officers with whom he worked, the police social

worker also had to come to terms with violence. People at times were personally abusive. He had to learn to handle feelings within himself of shock, anger and resentment.

After about two years of modestly successful work, the position of the police social worker recently lost its funding in a time of local economic crisis. Prior to this, the social work student placements had been discontinued. The main reason for this was that adequate time for student supervision was not available. This also was related partly to economic factors.

As of this writing the training component of the project continues, in the absence of any significant service aspect. The loss of the main service component is essentially a failure on the authors' part to sell the concept to high administrative officials. The authors regularly receive laments from patrol officers that they are back where they started from a few years ago, with no one to turn to in so many complicated social situations. There is hope that as the economy improves, one or more police social workers again will be available.

It is felt that the authors have established, through the graduate student social workers and the trained police social worker, the validity of the concept. Social workers can practice within the police setting, making a contribution to improved police service. The social worker's greatest acceptance came from the officer on the street. By being available at times of crisis, the police social worker can move in aggressively to make some dent in a pathological system.

Perhaps the most important function he served was that which we have described as "community broker." In this role he stood somewhat outside of each system. He used this position of non-alignment to evaluate and select those services most appropriate for the client he had seen. His task could perhaps be termed an extended referral. The procedure involved establishing the needs of the client, as they saw it, and then evaluating with them which services they could and would make use of. The process continued as the police social worker contacted the agency to determine if they might then accept this client. If necessary he then physically introduced the client into that system.

In practice the police social worker functioned much more

independently than the students. He rode in his own vehicle with a portable radio and an assigned dispatch number. He would, at times, work as a team member with officers; on other occasions as a consultant to them; and, in the majority of cases, as a recipient of referred cases from the officer. In this latter capacity much of his work became follow-up as well, and he often found himself working days as well as nights. In his last months on the job, he was critically overextended and badly needed help.

The project succeeded well in reaching some of the goals set. The officers on patrol found that the police social worker could be of help to them. His services were used. The complaints were of his not being even *more* available for referrals and patrol work.

The project did not succeed as well at educating the social service community to the problems of police service. For the most part the mental health professional remained ignorant of, or uninterested in, police service cases. Only in individual case contacts did the police social worker gain some understanding from his peers of the problems encountered on patrol.

When project staff spoke within the community, fellow professionals would express some immediate interest or concern. Such interest, however, was generally short-lived. It is felt that these professionals may have been intimidated by the number or complexity of the problems presented. Under these circumstances one could understand their retreat from the issues raised. It is far more pleasant to work with the client who wants and seeks help.

The theory of police social work is, the authors believe, a sound one. The police social worker in practice, however, remains somewhere on the fringes of respectability. He is neither fish nor fowl, neither traditional social worker nor real police officer. In the authors' experience the police social worker does fill an existing service vacuum within the community. He is in a position to enrich police service and to contribute to more effective community social service.

The police social worker has previously been discussed in an article in *Police Chief* magazine.[1]

---

[1]Brand, Dennis, Colbach, Edward, Euler, James, and Fosterling, Charles: "The Police Social Worker — a Community Broker." *The Police Chief, XLI,* Number 6, June, 1974, pp. 28-32.

Questions for Discussion

1. What do the authors suggest as to possible advantages of the police-social worker team on patrol?
2. Note and discuss changes that might occur with increased understanding by social service agencies of police service problems.
3. From the experiences of the police social worker in practice, were police officers put in additional danger by his involvement?
4. From the case examples provided, would you say the services of the police social worker were different in quantity or quality from those a police officer might have provided?
5. What do the authors suggest about crisis services available within the community at nights and on weekends?
6. Discuss ways in which you might initiate a police social work program in your police department.
7. What common myths do the authors suggest are held by social workers about police officers and by police officers about social workers?
8. In what types of cases might the police social worker be most useful and why?

Chapter VI

FEEDBACK FOR POLICE
FROM FRIENDS

POLICE officers often express concern about their relationships with the public. They say the public does not understand them. It does not appreciate the difficulty of the job police do. To the degree that there is lack of understanding, it is detrimental to good police-citizen communication. Without good communication police and citizenry cannot work together constructively. Too often it is assumed conveniently by the policeman and the citizen that the fault lies with the other, but communication requires effort on the part of all involved. In this chapter some of the factors contributing to poor communication and poor understanding between police and citizen will be discussed.

Following is a brief story, human and typical in many ways of both individual and organizational response to "criticism." It illustrates something of our oversensitivity and of our difficulty in acknowledging limitations.

JOHN

The following situation occurred between us (the authors) and a mutual friend, John. John is a great guy to be around — generous, fun-loving, dependable and bright. We knew him before his marriage, before the two children, and even before his current mortgage and job difficulties. John, like all of us, does have his blind spots.

John has had difficulty in his jobs. Bright, capable and hardworking as he is, he is forever losing them. He is a good worker. One could say almost *too* good. As he would explain, he often found ways to improve his job. He could do things more efficiently, "better" than the boss had asked for. His employers were not always as enthusiastic about this and obviously interpreted the situation much differently than he.

As one said, "John is smart all right, but just too damn big for his breeches. That's why I sent him on his way. There is room for only one boss in this job, and that's me."

This sort of thing happened to John a number of times and both his friends and family became more and more concerned. Finally, the two of us went over and sat down to have a talk with him.

One of us made a comment, "Look, John, you may be twice as smart as any man you've ever worked for, but you sure aren't going to keep a job by rubbing it in. What the hell are you trying to prove?"

This made sense to us, but *John* wasn't convinced. In fact he got a little angry and told us that we really didn't understand. Neither of us had ever worked in any of those jobs. What the hell did we know about trying to tell him something he had lived through? Those companies were all the same. The only guys who ever got promoted were the "yes" men. He was pretty sure that they even passed along information about him from one employer to the next.

The gist of it was that it was their problem, not his. John is pretty much like all of us. He could see clearly what he was doing and why he was doing it. He knows his intentions and purposes but must infer those of others. Being friends of his he accepted that we did wish to help him but still felt hurt and resentful towards us.

As with John the authors wish to assure police officers that criticisms are well intentioned. They are meant to be helpful and constructive. The authors acknowledge, as they had to with John, that they have indeed not worked in any one else's job.

It is suggested however, that the authors' program can offer something not available from within the system. A view from a different perspective is offered. Social workers are obviously not embroiled in the day-to-day problems and pressures of the policeman's job. They do not claim that their view is the correct one. The authors' perspective, however, may provide one more point from which to take a bearing and set a course. As with all travel through uncharted territory, the final destination is reached through bearings made from numerous locations, each in part correcting the errors of the former.

With no claim to infallibility, the authors see three main factors — isolation, control and immediacy — which limit good police-citizen communication, particularly as it affects "police service."

Isolation

What does it do to the individual? One example is the neighborhood recluse or hermit. Most officers have been called in because of problems arising around such an individual, a little old man or woman no longer in communication with the community and in all probability becoming more defensive and paranoid as the years go by. Stories spread, the person is feared and avoided. Kids sometimes throw stones at the house.

"Old Harry" will perhaps buy a gun to protect himself, and then someone may be injured or killed. It has happened in this community, and it probably has in many others. "Old Harry's" story is one example of what can happen through extreme isolation. Fear, misunderstanding and resentment tend to build on both sides. It takes effort to avoid such isolation or to break it down once it exists.

Many officers express feelings of isolation from the society they police. They see themselves as separate from the community and its social values. Some even express feelings of isolation from their own wives and families.

In some ways police systems seem to encourage and foster such isolation. The officer may work a shift that limits all social contacts other than with fellow officers. The separate identity by uniform and responsibility isolate and set the policeman apart. Group identity and loyalty can lead at times to the point of an "army of occupation" attitude. Loyalty under those circumstances is no longer to job and community but to the system or perhaps to fellow officers only. All others, including wife, family and friends, can then become "outsiders" and somewhat suspect.

Officers have often discussed this with the authors. Many express concern or displeasure about it. Some were complaining, some were bragging and others were doing a little of both. The

problems may come in dealing with others who are not members
of a select or initiated group. Do officers in their select capacity
still try to understand "outsiders," or do they expect only that
others try to understand us?

This issue of isolation is well illustrated by two typical and
often repeated statements. These statements can be used to explore this problem within the police system.

"Nobody really understands a police officer but another police
officer." There is an element of partial truth to this statement.
Pushed to its extreme, however, each officer might also admit,
"Nobody really understands me but me." It is true that each profession has its own demands and pressures uniquely understood
only by others within that profession. Be they doctors, ministers,
pimps or prostitutes, they all take pride in their ability to meet
these demands and pressures and to cope.

The officer on patrol, involved with a citizen in crisis, has too
significant an impact to be isolated or out of touch. Police isolation should not be tolerated by the police system nor by the citizenry with whom it works. The police system cannot afford to be
misunderstood by nor misunderstanding of its citizenry.

As one officer said in describing a problem in personal relationships, "I guess I used to want people to like me without knowing
me." This individual experience may parallel something of what
the whole police system goes through in its public relations.

There are other implications to the statement, "Nobody really
understands a police officer but another police officer." For some
it may be another way of saying, "I really don't have to think
about what you've said because you aren't a policeman." It is a
way of thus closing communication and ending discussion rather
than encouraging or expanding it. The reader may well remember those old, unsatisfactory platitudes from his childhood: "But
you've never been a mother," or, "When you get to be my age."

There is a danger for officers who use such a statement to close
their minds to new ideas. They may be defining professionalism
in terms of having answers. True professionalism is really the
dedication to seek answers and to ask the hard questions. Organizations which insist that only those ideas generated within the
system have value quite often end up determining that the only

thing that should be done is what is being done.

Another police isolationist statement often heard is, "Police work is police business."

Yes, it is. But social workers would also like to think that "Crime is everybody's business." When it is stated as police business, social workers tend to hear an unstated "and it's none of yours." The attitude says in part, "Just give us the men and equipment we asked for and leave us alone to do our job."

But can you really? Can the police system take total responsibility for crime? The authors think it would be foolish to do so. It is suspected that medicine will never solve illness. Welfare will never solve poverty. In reality we must accept that the ill, the poor, and the criminal will always be with us. Any group claiming total responsibility for such problems will be saddled with total blame when these problems are not solved.

One aspect of isolation is a heightened group loyalty. Like the flag and motherhood, loyalty is often seen as beyond criticism. There are some good aspects but a few negatives should be pointed out as well. Two other subgroup samples will be used as illustrations. Seminars have been held for some special groups. One was for a group of black men. These were men assigned to the police department in a rather tentative community relations program. To win acceptance, if that were possible, they thought they were being asked to abandon old loyalties for new.

A week-long seminar was scheduled for these men. The group met and set its own goals for the week. The men noted as problems for their group: their casual response to time, certain standards of dress and behavior that did not fit their new roles, and the disruptive behavior of some of the members. The supervisor, a member of the group, felt he was often sabotaged in his efforts to establish a workable operation. Others within the group cheerfully agreed this was so.

The group agreed that these were the problems that they needed to work on. This did not mean that they did work on them, however. They recognized them, acknowledged them and continued to act as usual. Sessions were disrupted, members straggled in late and all in the best of humor. It seemed to the authors that in each of these sessions that any man could claim the full tolerance of the group. None could, in comfort, impose limits on another, lest his claim for tolerance and brotherhood in the future be jeopardized.

Another group about whom the authors have some information are alcoholics. One organization using alcoholic helpers provided beds for skid row alcoholics with only the condition that no bottles be brought in. It was found, however, that the "alcoholic helpers" could not set such limits for their brother alcoholics.

What are the lessons of these two examples for police officers or any other isolated subgroup? In both groups discussed there was closeness and extreme tolerance, but often to the detriment of the group improvement.

Group loyalty within the police system can also mean the condoning and justification of whatever another police officer does. This can and does occur within the police system. This was observed in simple situations such as the video-taped training sessions. In these sessions officers respond to a simulated crime situation. The authors became aware and accepted as realistic that each officer would respond in individualized ways to the staged crime. After all, each officer has individualized capacities and differing ways of handling problems. The authors were fascinated, however, with the group response as each group assured themselves that however the officer had responded was the only way he could have as a policeman. Officer response was a "given." The variable was always in terms of the citizen, criminal or complainant. The same problem situations were often staged over and over again. The authors continued to be fascinated at the individual variations in handling problems and with the group consistency in protecting its officers from even a suggestion of criticism.

A more serious example of the danger of uncritical group loyalty was presented in one of the seminars comprised of officers from around the state. A young officer described a policeman known to him in the most negative terms. He described the man as a liar and a coward and told of instances where this officer had put other officers at risk of their lives. He went on, however, to claim his willingness to die for him if necessary based only on his "wearing the uniform." "Belonging" made that officer immune to criticism or corrections. Some others within the group were not as "understanding" nor as generous in their tolerance of this situation. This example and the issue of loyalty were hotly debated but were not resolved within the seminar group.

Isolation and an acceptance of answers only from within limit a group's ability to self-evaluate and self-correct. Options are drastically curtailed and learning is held back. The process then becomes, "We do it this way now because we have done it this way in the past."

Control

The issue of the police officer's responsibility for the control of others is another major area of officer concern. Officers see themselves as employed by society to enforce certain social controls. They see their ability to control situations as also necessary to their personal safety. Control can become to some officers a value in itself. Others transfer the concept from the control and enforcement of laws to the control and enforcement of social and moral standards. Some officers present themselves as employed to maintain the moral standards of the society.

The focus on control in this text will be in its effect within the police service area. One might ask how much of the control of another is actuality or myth. The authors have seen officers manipulated by citizens when the officers thought they were in control. One masochistic individual, for example, regularly goaded officers into abusing him verbally and physically.

One aspect of control is knowledge. The more one knows of a situation, the more one can control the circumstances and outcomes. What happens, however, when one moves into the complicated and involved areas of police service? There is a hodgepodge of facts, feelings, beliefs, and attitudes that almost defy sorting and organization. An officer can convince himself that he is in control only by oversimplifying the problem. If he can make complicated problems seem black and white, he feels better. This can only occur in his mind, however, since he cannot control reality by wishes.

Another complicating aspect of control is to gauge by some standard. The officer conceives of a right and proper way, some ideal position that must be reached. How adequate can that ever be for police service? Such situations are far too individual and too varied to be resolved in such a manner. Personal standards, no matter how clear or well intentioned, no matter how proper and right for one's own life, are of little use to others. Social workers are often pushed in their training to put forth "the correct way" of handling psychotics, family fights and the like. The authors try to do this, but with recommendations for maintaining common sense and flexibility in any method used.

The authors contend that the very concept of control can, at times, be both inefficient and ineffective. The officer who feels he controls others may well be deluding himself into a false feeling of security. It may be far more to his advantage to realize that none of us is ever guaranteed full control.

It would seem that in much of police service the issue of control might be best avoided. When one moves beyond the point of physical control into the area of human emotions, the very nature of the problem changes. To handle such matters well requires flexibility, sensitivity and openness — a willingness to listen and to hear.

The issue of self-control is also pertinent here. The authors have noted that officers experience much more psychological violence than physical. On the job there are constant assaults on the officers' emotional stability.

One officer told of being called out on a child drowning. The family lived in a houseboat on the river. A little girl of eight had gone out to feed the ducks and had not come back. The mother was in a state of shock after an elderly neighbor had run over to tell her of seeing the girl slip and fall into the water.

The police found the girl's body within a couple of hours. The primary officer involved had, he thought, handled the whole matter quite professionally. "It's all in a days work," he thought, after consoling the mother and taking care of the other details.

Almost a year later, however, his own daughter came near drowning in a neighborhood pool. The officer had great difficulty handling this. He had trouble sleeping, had nightmares and uncontrollable fits of shaking.

The earlier experience of the child drowning at the houseboat came back with great force. Apparently it effected him more than he was willing to admit at the time. At the advice of a fellow officer, he did seek some psychological counseling. Talking about it helped. "Just putting some of it into words was a great relief," he said later.

Self-control is one of the burdens placed upon the average police officer. He is expected to do the job and to not show feeling. He is perhaps even expected not to have feeling. Many of the officers that the authors have dealt with saw this as an expectation of fellow officers and of themselves as well.

Officers have brought this problem up in other forms. "We are taught a lot about the taking of physical risks but almost nothing about emotional risks." A police officer's job, however, entails many emotional risks. It is highly charged and emotionally stressful with many challenges to the officer's psychological stability.

It is suggested that officers be permitted and encouraged to express true feelings. Too often the experiences are shoved off by both the officer and his peers as "just part of the job." In doing so the system demands far more of the officer than it has a right to do.

Departments may well explore this in terms of its destructiveness to individual officers. They certainly appear to go through far more than their share of marital discord, divorce, ulcers, heart attacks and the like. Others may even deaden feelings through the use of alcohol.

Departments might think about debriefing after particularly stressful situations. Group discussions might be mandatory for officers who have shot another or have been injured themselves in the line of duty. Some local departments have begun to experiment in helping officers psychologically debrief traumatic incidents. If this is department policy, it is easier for the officer to admit he is troubled by such an occurrance.

Immediacy

Police officers constantly handle crisis situations. They move from crisis to crisis, doing what they can and often aware that nothing will be fully resolved by their intervention. They enter, involve themselves, resolve the crisis and leave, quite aware that the situation may well repeat itself next week or next month, identically or with some slight variation.

The authors suspect that officers may be too conditioned to immediacy. They have met officers who have lost their awareness of themselves and of their departments in any kind of a time frame. Each call was answered and resolved in its immediate context only.

Analysis of one call illustrates this point. On this call a very disturbed and potentially explosive individual was cleverly tricked out of his weapons. The situation was tentative and dangerous. The officers handled it quickly and efficiently. They made, however, two mistakes. The first was to leave this disturbed citizen with the feeling of having been deceived and belittled. The second was to consider this an immediate problem only.

Two weeks later other officers dealt with the same man, who was now in a far more angry mood. Fortunately no one was killed or injured. The situation, however, was much more tentative and risky the second time around.

If prevention becomes a police goal, police are going to have to be far less reactive in nature and much more cognizant of the part they can play to initiate change. Officers who will acknowledge that they treat citizens differently depending on the attitudes and behavior of the citizen toward them seem unaware that their attitudes and behavior will in turn influence the citizen.

This leads to another aspect of time. Much of the police focus is on the preparatory aspects of the work and on readiness. If you talk to a police officer about his police service interactions with the citizen, he will often contend that he has at the most five minutes to solve a problem. He must, he will say, be back in his car on the radio and in contact to answer other calls or backup a fellow officer. This has a profound effect on his willingness to involve himself deeply in any contact.

There is a local term called "Out of Service Time" (OST) which defines the time in which a police officer is out of his vehicle and in contact with a citizen. It is not known if this is a national term, but it does define to some extent what is understood to be a national attitude. What it says in essence is that service (work time) is within the police vehicle. It is when one is in contact with headquarters and available for duty, rather than when functioning in a police to citizen interchange, that one is working.

The effects of this are significant. They relate back to isolation, and certainly have their effects on depths of contact. If the object is to disengage oneself from the citizen contact and to patrol, it will mean a search for the quickest, most expedient and superficial resolution of a call possible.

It has meant that many techniques for communication are not mastered. They are not seen as valuable, productive or within the police sphere of responsibility. Even though these techniques are not time determined, they are defined as such. "We don't have the time to really communicate," is often said. Quality of communication in a relationship is not necessarily determined by the time involved. Seeing it as such, however, has kept many officers from realizing the value of good communication techniques.

In discussing what the authors see as problems — isolation, control, immediacy and the use of time — they do not wish to discount their reasons for existence. It is assumed that the police system as it presently functions has found some reason to emphasize these qualities. The purpose in discussing them here is to raise questions. They undoubtedly have purpose and benefit. In looking at the other side of the coin, however, they also have limitations.

The point which is of most concern here and throughout the authors' contact with the police system has been that of isolation. Many police officers, in discussing isolation, express the feeling that it could be solved by some public relations effort and the building of "image." It is felt that it is the person-to-person contact that has the most significant effect on attitudes, not "image building" through some public relations effort.

Feelings of trust come out of personal experience. The officer needs to be known to his community and by its citizenry. Police departments should use any methods they can devise to foster police-citizen interaction.

One example of this is the "ride-along program." In this program an officer takes a citizen along with him on patrol. Programs such as this do work. In talking with people who have accompanied an officer, one finds a growing respect for the difficulties of the job. Sharing an experience brings understanding as nothing else can.

The problems of society will not be solved by "departmental thinking" or by individual professional approaches. As well as learning from others, the police system has much to contribute from its knowledge of social problems within the community. The authors advocate a sharing of responsibility and a continued effort to work together.

Questions for Discussion:

1. What do the authors mean by police isolation?
2. How do the authors see the issue of control and police work?
3. What do the authors mean by immediacy?
4. Discuss the concept of Out of Service Time.
5. Are other societal systems isolated?
6. Should police officers be concerned with problem prevention?

Chapter VII

FEEDBACK FOR NONPOLICE
FROM NONPOLICE

A young man named Joe had had a tough life. He had the misfortune of being born into one of those families where chaos was usual. His parents were immigrants who never really felt comfortable in this country. His father always seemed to be out of work or in a job that afforded only a marginal subsistence. His chronically unhappy parents constantly picked at one another verbally, and occassionally his father would severely beat his mother. Joe remembered many awful nights from his childhood when he could hear his mother's quiet sobs after she had been beaten or insulted by his father. He often felt intense rage toward his father but did not know how to express it in any safe way. Usually he kept this rage in. It showed mainly in his poor school performance due to poor concentration. It also showed in the fact that he had a duodenal ulcer by the time he was fourteen.

Joe had two younger brothers, but he got little support from them. If anything, he felt competitive toward them, competitive for the little affection his parents could give. He did not fare too well in this competition. For one thing, he was extremely ugly physically. Everything about his face seemed to be distorted, with big ears that stuck out, one a bit lower than the other, a big, flat nose and very thick lips. All this was somehow set in a rather small, round head. His eyes especially looked grotesque, being rather puffy and with a Mongoloid slant. Added to all this was the fact that he was generally quite uncoordinated in all of his bodily movements. When he was seven a pediatrician remarked about him, behind his back but in a voice he overheard, that he had the "FLK syndrome." This is crude medical jargon for "funny looking kid." There appeared to be something wrong with him, but it was too nonspecific to be given any particular name.

129

If Joe had been as dull mentally as he looked, the unfortunate events of his life might not have had such an impact on him. But in fact he was extremely bright and extremely sensitive. He was usually quite miserable. Thus, he was a poor student in school. He barely passed some years of his grammar school experience.

He did manage to struggle through high school. After that he kind of dropped out. He let his hair grow long and grew a beard, giving him a bit of a "Jesus Christ" appearance. This also hid his face a bit. He drifted around the country awhile and experimented with a variety of drugs. Around his nineteenth birthday he returned to the metropolitan area where he was raised. He then presented himself to a local drug program for help.

He received psychological and vocational testing, and everyone was surprised at the high innate intelligence he demonstrated. Frightening, however, were the depth of his depression and his shakey hold on reality.

The department of vocational rehabilitation was able to arrange for financial aid so that he could enroll in a local community college to study electronics, a subject for which he had some aptitude. Money was also obtained so that he could be in weekly psychotherapy with a very competent clinical psychologist in private practice.

Joe met with this psychologist for ten months. These were a stormy ten months. He had such rage toward authority that he often left the psychologist's office before a session was over. He often threatened suicide as he left, leaving the psychologist with a very uncomfortable feeling that would disturb his sleep at night. The psychologist was never sure whether Joe would be alive for the next appointment. Occasionally Joe would call him at home, high on marijuana, and cry over the phone. The psychologist had Joe evaluated by a psychiatrist who recommended tranquilizers. Joe refused to take them.

During one session Joe cursed the psychologist, stating that the psychologist did not really care for him and was seeing him only for the money. Joe left early during this session, stating with special vehemence that the psychologist would never see him alive again. The psychologist struggled with his own feelings of anger and fear. He was sorry that he had ever taken Joe on as a patient. He partly wished that Joe would carry through his suicide threat. At this point he doubted that Joe could ever be successfully treated as an outpatient. He thought that Joe really needed long-term, intensive inpatient care at some institution like the Menninger Clinic or Chesnut Lodge. Financially this was impossible, of course.

This particular day the psychologist was very tired. He had had a succession of bad interviews, and he wondered if he could make it through his last one. He was struggling to regain his composure when his secretary came into his office with the news that Joe had apparently climbed out on a third floor window ledge and was threatening to jump. The psychologist followed his secretary's direction to the third floor. He found Joe not actually on a ledge but just staring out of a completely open window in the hallway. A crowd was beginning to gather in the hall as the psychologist approached Joe. He didn't get too close but tried to engage his patient in some conversation. Joe refused to answer and edged a bit closer to the window.

"Should I call the police?" someone asked.

"Hell, yes," the psychologist answered, his voice betraying both his anger and his fear.

In a few minutes two police officers appeared. "What should we do?" one asked.

"Take him to the county hospital. Commit him!" the psychologist said.

Joe suddenly seemed to relax a bit. "Wait, I'll just leave," he said.

"No way," the psychologist said. "Take him to the hospital," he said to the police. "Just get him out of here. He's a danger to himself." Partly he was talking out of concern for Joe, but partly he was talking out of anger. He just wanted to be rid of Joe.

One of the police officers shrugged and moved closer to Joe. "We're taking you to the hospital," he said softly. "Will you come peacefully or are we going to have a wrestling match?"

"I'll come peacefully," Joe answered, hanging his head and acting very subdued.

The tense scene ended as the officers quietly led Joe away.

That night the psychologist sought out one of his colleagues for an informal consultation. He was still very upset by the whole thing, but he had settled down enough to analyze the situation a bit. Had he made some mistakes in his handling of Joe both today and in the past? Was it really necessary to call the police, or had he just wanted to punish Joe a bit? The psychologist knew that the hospital would not keep Joe very long, if he had been accepted as a patient at all. He would soon have the problem right in his own lap again. He was in a hard business. He did feel very grateful to the police, however, for they had in a sense temporarily rescued him from Joe.

It was coincidental that a few days later this same psychologist was contacted by us regarding another patient with whom he had dealt.

We (the authors) are often looking for patients to be interviewed by one of our police classes. We thought this particular patient would be a good subject to interview. We asked for the psychologist's permission to approach the patient about performing a community service by telling his story to a group of police. We expected it would also be good for this patient to meet with the group. It has been our experience that most patients are treated very kindly by our students and usually get a good feeling from participating.

The psychologist responded instantly, with some irritation in his voice. "No. What business have a bunch of cops got prying into my patient's private life? Besides, it might reinforce in him the idea that he has a bad problem."

The point of this long story is obvious. Forty-eight hours before, when this psychologist was in trouble with a patient, he readily called upon the police for help. In one of the compartments of his mind, the police were, in a sense, his colleagues. In another compartment they were aliens seeking to "pry" into his patient's life.

Is it any wonder that police have antagonism toward such contradictory attitudes? Was the psychologist right or wrong? Or is there no such thing as clear right or wrong in this complicated area being discussed here.

This chapter will be directed primarily to those people who are not police but who have important interaction with many of the same people that police deal with. The authors introduce here what might be termed the unofficial "hate list" of police. This list includes judges, lawyers, doctors (especially psychiatrists), psychologists, social workers (often seen as being synonymous with welfare workers), teachers and ministers. These people are often considered to be incredibly naive and unrealistically tolerant by police, who describe them as "bleeding heart liberals." The people on this list, according to police, do not have a very deep understanding of the inherent rottenness of many humans and, therefore, do not treat them with appropriate disdain and toughness. The police think they have been abandoned by the people on their hate list. They make decisions that deeply affect the police but never bother to ask their advice and are not around to back them up when these decisions prove to be wrong.

Rather than to criticize this somewhat slanted attitude by police, this chapter will attempt to explore its origins and to examine any justifications for it. The main thrust of this chapter will be to chide a bit those nonpolice who have, in a sense, deserted police.

The trend in society today is to keep people out of institutions such as mental hospitals and prisons. Or, when a person is in such an institution, to get him out as soon as possible. This philosophy is based on America's belief in individual freedom and human dignity. This philosophy is certainly sound as long as careful selection is made and as long as the community has adequate follow-up facilities. If not, the brunt of the inadequacies will often fall upon the low man on society's authority totem pole, the policeman.

Some of the police complaints seem valid to us, while others appear to be the result of their own isolation and narrowness of outlook. The authors do believe, however, that it is the responsibility of nonpolice, often better educated and better paid, to first listen nonjudgementally to police and then to reach out to them to bridge the gap.

After the program had been in operation for about eighteen months, Dr. Edward M. Scott asked us to write a chapter about our work for a book he was editing on criminal rehabilitation. This book, entitled *Criminal Rehabilitation ... Within and Without the Walls*, was published in 1973.[1] The chapter was

---

[1]Colbach, E., and Fosterling, C.: Police and the mental health professional: A case of desertion. In Scott, E. (Ed.): *Criminal Rehabilitation...Within and Without the Walls.* Springfield, Thomas, 1973, pp. 178-195.

entitled "Police and the Mental Health Professional: A Case of Desertion." It was directed primarily at colleagues in the mental health field. We felt strongly then, as now, that the police role in mental health care is too often downgraded and overlooked by our colleagues.

So many of the statements directed to mental health people, then, are also applicable to those in other fields. It is worthwhile here to restate some of the main points.

Police have had more than their share of "expert" lectures from people in other disciplines. Though these experts may be well-intentioned, they often have little real knowledge of what the police officer faces on the street. Over and over again the authors have advised people who would work with the police to become students again, and the best first grade classroom is a patrol car. The authors have called patrol car riding a *sine qua non* for anyone interested in working better with the police.

Ample documentation of the policeman as a helper has been offered. Mazer has written of those people who express their emotional difficulties primarily in acts and disordered life styles.[2] He has included in these "parapsychiatric events" such things as fines, jail sentences, probation, juvenile delinquency, marital dissolution, premarital pregnancy, some automobile accidents, auto license withdrawal, alcohol problems, suicide attempts and suicide.

It is the contention of the authors that as he struggles to deal with such problems, the police officer is often deserted by the rest of us. This desertion takes different forms.

One form of this desertion is in the minimal communication between police and others involved in managing these so-called "parapsychiatric events." So many of the other managing agencies are open only during "normal working hours." As has been pointed out throughout this book, this is often when the least is happening.

We have also mentioned the unwillingness of many agencies to reach beyond their walls to deal with the "unmotivat-

---

[2]Mazer, M.: Two ways of expressing psychological disorder: The experience of a demarcated population. *American Journal of Psychiatry, 128*:933-938, 1972.

ed" people who will not come in to ask for help.

A last form of desertion, and perhaps the worst, is the quickness with which some criticize police handling of various situations. Police always contend that one must be a policeman to know what it is really like on the street. Perhaps this is a bit of an extreme position, but certainly it is presumptuous to criticize from an office or courtroom what a police officer does on the street unless one has a good idea of the pressures he faces there.

Police officers are usually very responsible people. They find it hard to understand how it is that they are so often left alone on the firing line with little actual or moral support from the rest of the community. And yet so many mental health workers say that they care, that they are in "helping" professions. If so, a police officer asks, "Why aren't you involved in the same kind of problems I am at the times I am? Isn't your absence a form of irresponsibility?" There is a credibility gap, and this partly accounts for the poor record of police referral to other community agencies.

The police officer feels deserted by so many of the people whose decisions have an impact on his job at the street level. Numerous examples of this can be taken from case files. The authors would like to share some of these cases with the reader.

ARMED ROBBERY

A young man grew up in a very difficult home situation. His father left his mother for another woman when the subject of this story was only two years of age. Another man soon moved in with the mother, and two more children followed. This common-law stepfather never liked the young boy, and during his frequent drinking bouts he was quite abusive to him. He swore at him and beat him with a belt for very minor misbehaviors. The mother tried to intervene but was usually ineffective.

As might be expected the young boy had a variety of adjustment problems as he grew up. He suffered from nightmares, he wet the bed until he was twelve and he was a poor student at school. He was described as being hyperactive. Various teachers recommended some sort of counseling, but the family never was interested. The stepfather was a logger, and the family moved around a lot which further compounded the young man's problems. He was forever getting used to new schools and friends.

By the age of ten he was an accomplished petty thief. He would go through the desks and lockers of his schoolmates and take whatever he could. At the age of eleven he stole one hundred dollars from a teacher's purse. Whenever he was exposed he was brought before his parents, who seemed embarrassed and befuddled. He especially enjoyed seeing the look of embarrassment on his stepfather's face. This alone was enough for him to continue, despite the beatings he would then receive at the man's hands.

By the age of fourteen the subject was burglarizing homes and stealing cars. He spent two years in and out of various reform schools but to no avail. At the age of seventeen, by now a high school dropout with no job skills, he left home for good and committed his first armed robbery. He was caught near the scene after firing some shots at the arresting officer. A psychiatric report described him as an extremely angry young man with very poor behavior controls. He was called an antisocial personality.

He spent the next three years in a state correctional institution. He was out six months, entered into an unsuccessful marriage, began to drink heavily, and was apprehended in the commission of another armed robbery. Again there was a shootout between him and the two officers first on the scene. Luckily, however, no one was hurt.

Another presentence psychiatric exam revealed him to be a severe antisocial personality. The examining psychiatrist said he knew of no feasible means of changing this behavior pattern. He even added that in some ways the subject felt more comfortable in institutions. There his aggressiveness could be controlled. There he did not have to face up to the kind of daily twentieth-century stresses that he just was not emotionally equipped to handle.

The presiding judge was sufficiently frightened of this subject's danger to society that he gave him, at the age of twenty-one, a long prison sentence. He did well in prison, seemingly enjoying the routine. He clearly proved that he could adjust well in a prison setting. As a reward he was paroled to see if he could do likewise in society after seven years of incarceration.

In less than six months he proved that he could not. He had trouble holding a job, he entered into another unsuccessful marriage, he drank heavily to deal with the anxiety he felt, and he committed another armed robbery. Coincidentally he was apprehended after the robbery by one of the very same officers who had arrested him seven years before. This time there was no shootout, and he seemed quite docile as he was stopped. He attracted police attention because he was driving his car in a very erratic manner, apparently being drunk.

But it was not over. He was charged with armed robbery in the first degree. The defense said he was too drunk to form an intent to commit first degree armed robbery. A psychiatric expert witness testified to that effect. A state psychiatrist, of course, testified differently.

That particular jury had made some strange decisions previously, and the state felt that an acquittal was possible. The state psychiatrist said privately that if the subject was acquitted, he had no doubt he would soon do something even more convincing to get back to prison. The psychiatrist said he unconsciously wanted to go back, although he could not consciously admit this to himself.

When the arresting police officer heard of the district attorney's apprehensions, he muttered to his partner, "Next time I'll waste the bastard, whether it's next week or in seven years. But I'm not going through this again."

As it turned out the man was found guilty and given a long prison sentence once more. When he will be out again is another matter.

Obviously something is wrong here. This case is not unique. Every big city courthouse has cases like this regularly. First, there was a parenting failure. Following this, there was a failure of the criminal justice system to rehabilitate. With the history presented, is this young man at all salvageable? Should he ever again be allowed out of prison? What business have psychiatrists got in being involved in such legal technicalities? Does the defense attorney have any responsibility to society at large, beyond his responsibility to his client?

The answers to these complicated questions often appear obscure. But the questions have to be asked over and over; something is wrong. What really disturbs the police officer is when he does not hear these questions being asked, when people seem quite satisfied with the way things are. He is not satisfied because he knows something is wrong. He does the real dirty work, and he knows.

NOT GUILTY BY REASON OF INSANITY

A baby had the misfortune of being born into a family where there was serious mental illness. His mother had a series of nervous breakdowns and was diagnosed as suffering from chronic paranoid schizophrenia. The young child was raised primarily by a maternal aunt who helped the father as much as she could. She, however, was also unstable, and the mother was around enough to keep things in a constant state of turmoil. He was a very tense youngster.

Still he did adequately. He was bright and performed well in school, which gave him a lot of gratification. He did have trouble making friends and stayed a lot to himself, reading and daydreaming. He completed high school and even two years of college before dropping out because he felt a strong sense of isolation on a college campus. Everyone seemed to be having a good time except him.

He got a clerical job in an office and moved into a boarding house run by an elderly lady. Strange things began to happen to him. Something seemed very wrong with the world around him. He could not be specific, but he began to believe that he had a special mission to somehow "right" the world. One night he actually heard the voice of God speaking to him. "You, like my Son, are special." the voice said. "You, like Him, will die for the world's sins. But first you must do justice to the evil ones."

He did not at first understand that remark about doing justice to the evil ones, but gradually it became clear to him. One of the evil ones obviously was his landlady. There was something ominous about the way she looked at him. He decided that she would be the first of the evil ones to die. So, one night he crept into her bedroom and stabbed her repeatedly over her heart. The knife he chose was too big and too weak, and it kept getting caught in her rib cage. Her screams brought help. Though she was in critical condition, she survived.

A number of psychiatrists interviewed the young man, and their findings were unanimous. He was suffering from acute schizophrenia, probably partly inherited from his mother and partly due to the trauma of being raised by her. His thinking was illogical, the basic malady in this disease. This meant that he did not appreciate the wrongfulness of his conduct and could not conform his conduct to the requirements of the law. The court found him not guilty by reason of insanity. He was committed to the security ward of the state mental hospital for an indefinite period of time.

He was placed on large doses of phenothiazine medication, and the powerful tranquilizing effects of the drugs gradually cleared up his delusional thinking. Within six months time he appeared quite normal to the casual observer, and the doctors at the hospital said his acute schizophrenia was in remission. He would probably be all right if he stayed on his medication and lived in a somewhat protected environment. His attorney arranged for him to get his medication at the local county mental health clinic and arranged for him to live in a boarding house that catered to former mental patients.

After a court hearing during which all this was discussed, the judge somewhat reluctantly discharged the subject from the state hospital. It seemed as if the services available to the subject might keep him out of future difficulties. In fact the services were more like "pretend" services.

The boarding house he was living in was rather loosely supervised, and there was not nearly enough attention available to him. The county mental health clinic was willing to supply him with medication, but there was no capacity for reaching out to him when he stopped coming in after a few months. And the defense attorney who was going to supervise this program really had little true understanding of the serious nature of the subject's illness, seeing things on a rather superficial level. He was soon much too involved in his other, newer cases to pay much attention to following up on this one.

It was the subject's mother, of all people, who contacted the court to say that she thought her son was going downhill again. The judge ordered the man taken into custody, and in fact an examination showed that his delusional system was returning. He was lonely, discouraged about not making friends or finding a job, and he had stopped taking his medicine because he did not think he needed it.

The problem here is not that this man's situation cannot be

managed outside of an institution. It can be, if the services are
really there and not just "pretend" services. But real services are
expensive and complicated and not at all easy to provide.

What does the arresting policeman think when he follows cases
like this? Will telling him all the intricacies of a multipluralistic
system relieve him of his contempt for the court and mental
health systems? If the services are not really there, why must everyone pretend that they are.

THE DRUG CONFERENCE

For a few years in this locality there was a large, week-long
conference on drug abuse. This conference was attended by
people from all walks of life, including physicians, teachers,
ministers, mental health people, pharmacists and policemen.
This large conference had as many as five hundred people in
attendance. They all met in a large auditorium for formal
presentations and then later broke up into small groups for
discussions. Almost all of the formal presentations were given
by people who had a doctorate, either an M.D. or a Ph.D. These
"experts" would proceed to tell everyone else about the
intricacies of the drug abuse problem. Each year the police
contingent would attend dutifully and become more and more
angry as the week progressed. The formal speakers acted as if
they alone really had the facts, and there were even some
occassional snide remarks about the police outlook or
involvement in one situation or another. In their small groups
the police would complain that they had no spokesman at the
conference to represent their view. In the problem of drug abuse,
they were the real front-line troopers. Didn't anybody care to
hear what they had to say? They listened to statistics about
marijuana, for example. It seemed as if there were data to the
effect that marijuana use did not lead to hard drug abuse.
Therefore, marijuana laws and their rigorous enforcement were
too harsh. Maybe so, the police said, but that was different from
their experience. Didn't anybody care about their experience,
even if they didn't know how to use a chi square formula or how
to make statistically valid observations? Didn't their "clinical"
observations mean anything?

Every year it was suggested to the people who organized the

conference that it might be interesting to hear "the police viewpoint on drug abuse," if such a consensus could be reached. Every year these suggestions were ignored.

True, the police are partly to blame here. They are not the best of public relations people and tend to disdain that role. They often seem to hold others in such contempt that they do not put themselves out too much to communicate. Partly they may be afraid, being aware that there are people much better educated than they. Also they do not have easy access to the department's voluminous data. The police experience in so many areas is so pertinent to the universal problems in society. Yet, there is no easy way to get at the data. Their data systems are often not very sophisticated and the data not easily retrievable.

An example of this is a case of a man recently released from a mental hospital who visited his wife's place of employment and kidnapped her at gunpoint. This was recorded in the crime statistics as a kidnapping. There was no way of recording the fact that the kidnapping was done by a man with a history of considerable emotional conflict.

But do those who are nonpolice really give the police credit for learning anything from their intense, daily human experience? Is a policeman's opinion really worth hearing?

A CASE OF MURDER

Recently in one of the local papers there was a story about a man who had been found not guilty by reason of insanity for stabbing a relative. He was sent to the state mental hospital where he remained on the security ward for about six months and then was transferred to one of the more open general wards. He was on heavy medication and had shown improvement from his psychotic condition. He walked away from this general ward and turned up a few months later in a neighboring state after killing three people.

This story resembles somewhat the story of the man who stabbed his landlady. Such stories are not uncommon. Anyone who works in the field or reads the papers regularly knows of a number of similar episodes. Who should be criticized here? Perhaps the state hospital people should be criticized for letting this man leave the security ward. Their problem is that they have only limited beds on the security ward, and people have to be moved from that ward to other wards to make room for the influx. And they probably are not going to get many more beds on the security ward. This is the era of "community psychiatry," or the "Fourth Psychiatric Revolution." This is the trend to close down the state hospitals and to reintegrate people into the community. As stated before this is a decent concept, if the community resources are available. Often they simply are not.

Everyone in the field of mental health has had the experience of trying very hard to keep someone out of the hospital through large doses of medication, frequent office contacts, home visits, day programs and the like. For some people, however, the effort required is so enormous that the treating personnel give up in exhaustion and decide to utilize the hospital route.

The authors have had about thirty years experience in the field of mental health. They believe that some people may need to stay in a protective hospital setting forever, unless such extreme measures as prefrontal lobotomy or constant one-to-one supervision are employed. Protection is necessary for the community and for the sake of the individual. It certainly cannot be good for one's mental health to allow one's aggression to get out of control to the extent of hurting someone else.

In the face of the social movement and attitude called community mental health, who is again asked to do the dirty work when funds and manpower do not stand behind the movement? Who arrested this murderer the first time, and who arrested him the second time? What do you think those arresting policemen think about community mental health?

ALCOHOLIC SHOOTING

A man from a very disturbed home grew up to be a very angry, explosive individual. He was in trouble with juvenile authorities as a teenager. He enlisted in the U. S. Army but could not adapt to the discipline. He served some time for an armed robbery in his early twenties. He also had a bad marriage at that time. In his late twenties he became involved in an auto theft ring and again served some time in the penitentiary. When he got out he again failed at marriage.

Throughout much of his life, he drank when he was stressed. As one failure followed another, his alcohol intake increased. By the age of thirty-five he was an alcoholic, who consumed large quantities of whiskey daily. Whenever he drank he became aggressive and had frequent barroom fights. One day he had a barroom argument with a prostitute and left the bar in a rage. He found that his car had been wedged in at the curb by another car that had parked too close. He was kicking at the car that had him wedged in when its owner appeared. There was some heated discussion back and forth. Then the main subject of this story took a gun from his own car and severely wounded the man who had wedged him in. He erratically fled from the scene, smashing both cars as he maneuvered his car free.

The police were called, and later that night they apprehended the man after a chase. A careful investigation was done and all the facts seemed clearly to point to a conviction for attempted murder.

When the trial began, however, the involved policemen were not so sure. A defense psychiatrist argued that the man was so intoxicated that he could not form an intent to commit murder. As proof of this the defense brought into court videotape films of the man under the influence of alcohol. These films had been made in a hospital setting, with the man given alcohol in a controlled environment to study its effect upon him. On the films he did become quite irrational. The jury was impressed and acquitted him. He was thus completely free.

Again this is the American system of justice, and it is one of the best there has ever been. But what about the incredulous police response upon hearing that the man was turned loose? Who will have to respond to the call the next time he causes trouble? The question has to be asked again about the responsibilities of the defense attorney and the defense psychiatrist. Of course, they were just doing their job, as was the jury, but is that enough? Perhaps some elements of our judicial system need some serious rethinking. Some people believe the main issue to be determined at a trial is whether the accused committed the offense or not. If this is established, then maybe the experts, such as psychiatrists, can help the court decide what to do with the defendant.

THREATS TO KILL CHILDREN

One last story in this regard will be presented. A somewhat
unstable woman was deserted by her husband, who ran off with
another woman. She became quite depressed, did not eat and
had trouble sleeping. She went to her minister who really felt
the problem was a bit over his head, especially when she began
to talk of killing herself and taking her three children with her.
He referred her to a local mental health clinic, where a
psychologist met with her. He became convinced that she
should go into a hospital, but she refused to consider it. He
pushed this point and she ran from his office in a panic. He was
alarmed for the safety of the children, and he contacted a local
police agency. A policewoman went out to investigate, and the
disturbed lady called her lawyer. She did have some financial
assets and could afford a private attorney. The attorney
immediately took his client's side, feeling that there really was
not all that much wrong with her. He dismissed her threats to
hurt herself and her children as just idle talk to get attention. So
here the policewoman was caught in the middle, with the
psychologist telling her on the phone that he thought the
situation was potentially dangerous and the attorney at the
house making threats about lawsuits if the woman or her
children were harassed by the police. The policewoman asked
the psychologist to come out to the home, but he refused,
especially when the attorney made some threats about suing
him.

Some neighbors came by and got involved also. They
privately told the policewoman that they thought the lady
needed help but would not say it openly, since "they didn't want
to get involved."

Put yourself in the policewoman's place. It's late evening and
you have to sift through all this information and deal with a
threatening attorney. It would be easy to turn your back on the
whole thing and forget it. But police are usually too responsible
to do that. This policewoman would not have slept well that
night if she had done that. She persisted. She contacted a judge
and got a warrant to remove the children. The next day she met
with the psychologist and a neighbor and convinced them to

sign papers at the probate court so that the mother could have a mental hearing. This hearing took place, and the woman was committed. Her lawyer gave the policewoman and the psychologist a bad time at the hearing, however. Eventually she got over the worst of her depression and got her children back.

Here, once again, the police officer was caught in the middle. A mental health professional thought the lady needed help. A neighbor thought so also. Yet they were afraid of too much involvement, especially after a threatening lawyer began to vigorously protect what he considered to be his patient's rights. Only the policewoman's courageous persistence saved a possible disaster. How often are we all afraid to get involved, to leave it "to George." George often wears a police uniform, and he deeply resents so often having to go it alone.

What lessons may be learned by those of us who are not police from the preceeding stories? The following is offered as a discussion of those lessons.

First of all, many of us get overspecialized and do get isolated from life outside our own frame of reference. There is both an individual and a system isolation. The individual attorney, or the individual psychiatrist, for example, tends to see things a certain way. The attorney may be completely dedicated to the preservation of his client's rights. He may see everyone who walks through his door to be in need of his protection from a hostile world that wants to do harm to his client. The psychiatrist may feel quite comfortable working in his nicely decorated office, but how does he feel about leaving it? He can work well with verbal, motivated patients who come to him, but how about the rest of the world? Do either of the men in these examples look carefully at the broader world beyond their own little world?

Let's face it. We all wear professional blinders. Anyone, including the authors, who does not recognize this is a fool. The only saving grace for any of us is to be eternally aware of this and eternally vigilant and examining of ourselves.

We lose sight of the fact that others have value too. The police officer may not have all our degrees or our supposed level of sophistication, but maybe he knows some simple procedures for helping people that we have long since forgotten or have never learned in the first place. Some of his observations and techniques might be quite valid, and they should be given some credence.

Every agency too has a certain professional blindness. Every agency has a clear idea of the kind of people it likes to help, "the good client" or "the good patient." Each system becomes isolated itself. One almost universal attitude found among nonpolice systems is that police are somehow not part of that system: They are not helpers; they are "the enemy."

Why this overspecialization and isolation? There are probably many reasons. All of us are limited in this rigorous twentieth century America as to just how much stress and information our minds and personalities can handle. So, just to survive there is the need to place limits on what we do and what we think.

Our society also prizes individuality. Despite trends toward what might be called socialism, America remains a very individualistic society. We prize the individualist, whether it be a person or an agency. "If we can do it alone, let's do it that way," is a currently favored philosophy.

Being a specialist also leads to a certain feeling of competence. Our world is so complicated that we can not handle it *all* in the best manner. There are simply too many pressures brought to bear on the individual today. By narrowing our focus we can become specialists in one area and at least feel competent there. Man is insecure by nature, and the compulsive perfectionism of specialization at least belies a little bit our terrible fallibility.

Also, in this society, we rate social value by monetary income. The more money one gets for a job, the more status it (and he) has. Traditionally the job of a policeman has been a low-paying one. Therefore, it receives low status and respect.

This chapter has presented failures of the system. It has not presented success stories. The police officer, however, deals mostly with failures. He knows little of the successes, and he becomes embittered. He is "the low man on the totem pole." Is it any wonder that he begins to see the rest of us as "naive jerks"? Whose responsibility is it to reach out to him and somehow help him in dealing with the system's failures? The authors believe that the responsibility rests with those who have more status and power than he.

We need to speak out more clearly about what we really can do and what we cannot do. Is it a crime to admit that there are many hopeless cases in our society, people for whom we have no effective treatment or rehabilitation? How many good programs have been discredited and destroyed because people are fed into them who do not have a prayer of making much progress toward resocialization?

The authors have presented these cases of failure not to create nihilism but to encourage realism. Everyone has a responsibility to be a guardian of reality, first and foremost. In helping us to appreciate just what is reality and what is hopeful fantasy, the authors believe that the policeman has much to contribute. Policemen should be encouraged to speak out and mental health workers should listen much more carefully than they have to what he has to say. The policeman is valuable to all of us who are trying to make our society a better place.

Questions for Discussion

1. What "professional blinders" do you have?
2. Is there such a thing as "the hopeless case" in society?
3. Have you ever turned your back on police when you might have been helpful to them?
4. Do nonpolice make many efforts to understand police?
5. Are you afraid of police?
6. Do police have a right to be considered part of the helping system?
7. Do the authors come across as "ultraconservative" or "antiliberal" in this chapter?
8. Does the concept of "an unofficial police hate list" sound too far fetched?

Chapter VIII

THE FUTURE:
AUTHORITY AND SURVIVAL

"WESTERN civilization reached its peak in about 1910. Since then it has been all downhill with America leading the way." We were startled to hear a policeman in one of our classes say this recently.

When asked to elaborate, he said that it was at about this time when the individual's rights began to seriously conflict with society's rights. The individual was valued too highly and society not enough. As a result, the machinery designed to protect society from its irresponsible members has become increasingly complex and impotent. People are able to get away with anything, even murder, he said. Discipline is dead. It is only a matter of time before a more ordered society, like Communist China, rolls over us.

These sentiments are often heard from police. This specific statement came soon after the Communist victory in Vietnam, and it was particularly sobering. In working closely with police, it is hard not to be in sympathy with such attitudes. From their vantage point there are so many dangerous and destructive characters free in society that it seems as if the world will soon be engulfed by them. It is hoped that this officer is wrong, but at times we have done some troublesome wondering. Can a democracy such as ours really survive? What is the role of authority in our society?

In this last chapter we will try to review briefly the main points of the previous chapters and also make a few new ones.

We wish, in these final pages, to take a look at the role we think authority must play in society's future and its survival. It is firmly believed that authority is necessary. The masses of people

148

living on this planet, and the numbers in this country, cannot survive if each is left to do his "own thing." Humanity's need to band together in some structured society is as old as man himself. Common sense and our own deep instincts make us quite unsympathetic to blanket "antiauthority" stands.

At the same time, however, it is necessary for authority to be responsible to the people served. Cases of irresponsible authority abound. Police officers decry the fact that society has become too soft, saying that the police ought to be given a free hand "to clean things up." The authors recommend that such officers read Aleksandr Solzhenitsyn's *The Gulag Archipelago*. This book demonstrates well the dangers of uncontrolled authority.

As we see it, the real challenge for all authority, whether that authority be a parent or a president, is to learn to listen, to understand and then to take the best possible course of action for those concerned.

This book has focused on the police and their supporting systems. This last chapter deals primarily with the authority represented by this group of people.

"The police are the public and the public are the police" is part of a quote attributed to Sir Robert Peel in 1829.[1] The entire statement reads: "The police at all times should maintain a relationship with the public that gives reality to the historic tradition that the police are the public and that the public are the police, the police are the only members of the public who are paid to give full-time attention to duties which are incumbent on every citizen in the interest of community welfare."

The statement "the police are the public and the public are the police" ought to be repeated over and over again by all of us. The authority that the police have is given to them by the rest of the public. But such an investiture does not mean that the public has abdicated its responsibility or that the police can arbitrarily choose their own path.

What Peel said is that we all must be concerned about the community welfare. Not all of us, however, can devote our entire

---

[1]The Task Force on Policing in Ontario. Report to the Solicitor General, Ontario, Canada. February, 1974. Introduction.

working day to such community service work. Therefore, we hire police.

This sort of thinking is applicable, for example, to the common police complaint that they should be freed up from their "social work" so that they can devote themselves more to "criminal work." Who has determined that the police job is doing "criminal work" rather than "social work"? Certainly not the public, which continues to demand police involvement in both areas, to the degree that they can be delineated.

Emergency room physicians often complain that many of the people who come to emergency rooms are not having "real emergencies," and that they should be treated in doctors' offices during normal working hours instead. Who should be deciding how an emergency room is utilized, the doctors or the public they serve? Probably the most sensible answer is in this resigned statement by one physician, "An emergency room patient is defined as a patient who has arrived at the emergency room for help."

For police to be responsible authorities, we feel that they first have to recognize the fact that they do have a caseload. Then they must do all they can to get the training necessary to listen, to understand and to properly respond to their caseload. This is what programs such as ours are all about.

Throughout this book the authors have made some reference to the extended training they are now doing with the police. It took a number of years before we could gain the acceptance necessary to attempt this in this area. But the acceptance has come.

Currently we are working intensively with twelve police officers from the Multnomah County Sheriff's Department. We are working with these individuals a minimum of three hours weekly and will continue to do so for a total of at least one year. The extension of this program into a second year is quite possible. Their students are people from the patrolman to the lieutenant level who have demonstrated a special aptitude for and interest in the service aspects of police work.

Our goal is to help them become mental health paraprofessionals. To accomplish this we are using a basic psychiatric textbook as a foundation.[2] Again making ample use of actual patients and the local mental health agencies, we are emphasizing learning through experience. Only one's imagination limits what can be done. For example, the group interviewed a young man who was struggling back from a serious psychotic break. The plan is for the group to continue to meet with him at regular intervals, both to study his progress and perhaps to lend a helping hand in such areas as aiding him to find a better living situation and in finding work.

Another man, so depressed he lost interest in living, is involved in a regular ridealong program with group members as a part of his day treatment schedule.

It is hoped that as a result of this long-term training, these men will have a special feeling for mental health. They can help in bridging the gap between the mental health and police professions. It is also hoped that they can later assume the responsibility for training others in their department without outside help.

The authors do not envision a future when every police officer will be a professional psychologist or psychiatric social worker. We do, however, envision a time when such professionals will be an integral part of the operations division of every forward thinking police department. The model described in the chapter on the police social worker is a workable one. It is not the only one, as nothing is ever the *only* model to follow. But it did work for us.

In summary, it is felt that, regarding police authority, such authority in the future must become more responsive to the service demands the public makes on it. This can be accomplished by better police training in these areas and by departments employing professional mental health and social service people to work alongside the uniformed officer on the street.

This implies, of course, that such mental health workers also give some recognition to what police do and involve themselves in this work. The authors have given enough examples in this book to indicate that police are not the only ones who have to undergo some attitude change. Why should not most community

---

[2]Ulett, George: *Synopsis of Contemporary Psychiatry,* 5th edition. C.V. Mosby and Co., St. Louis, 1972.

agencies be on call at all times, just as the police are?

We would also like to say something about the authority system represented by judges, attorneys, various corrections people and the like. Men and women from these professions do not know enough about human behavior either, and because of this they make unrealistic demands and have unrealistic expectations for changes of behavior. They often let the police and the rest of the community down.

There is a general lack of understanding of how hard it is for human patterns of behavior to be changed. How hard is it to stop smoking, or to eat a little bit less, or to exercise a bit more? *Very hard* is the only answer. How much more difficult it is to change behavior patterns that are a bit more complicated, such as spending more time with your children or being a bit less dictatorial with your wife.

Anyone who has struggled in therapy, either as a patient or a therapist, knows how persistent and resistant to change the core aspects of our personalities are. This says a lot, of course, about the importance of early personality formation, of preventive programs for young children and young parents. Here is hope for the future.

In the authors' experience, authority usually looks upon the rights of natural parents to rear their children as they see fit as sacred. Because of this right we have seen children returned to terribly destructive home situations time and time again. So many of these antisocial problems are passed on from generation to generation. Do the child and the society that will eventually have to deal with him as a crippled adult have some rights too?

Of most pertinence here is the fact that the officer on the street often deals with the failed end product, the crippled personality who is on a repetitive, destructive path that no one can change. Is this viewpoint pessimistic or realistic? Only you can decide.

If this viewpoint has some realism to it, and if a person demonstrates danger to society with little capacity for change, should he not be removed from society? Maybe he should receive not five years, or ten years, or twenty years, but an indeterminate number of years.

The authors speak here of the indeterminate sentence. A person is sentenced to remain out of society until it can somehow be demonstrated that he is safe to return to it. Theoretically, a purse snatcher might spend a lifetime in jail for his offense, while a murderer may spend only a few years.

The problems of such a system, of course, are very great. How does a person demonstrate he is safe? Who makes the decisions? Has behavioral science demonstrated that good a capacity for prediction? How does one run a prison system when no one knows who will get out or when? And is not the whole idea un-American?

If one looks at the "track record" of a twenty-two-year-old young man who started petty thievery at the age of five and has now progressed to armed robbery, violent rape and murder, will a few years in prison change this behavior pattern?

The idea of the indeterminate sentence is a complicated one. But it is an idea that should not be quickly rejected. Authority must struggle to become more responsive to *all* of the society it serves. It seems to us that the pendulum of individual rights is swinging out to an extreme. It is now getting too far from the point representing the rights of society as a whole.

Perhaps an indeterminate sentence is too unfair and too risky in a democracy. Certainly prisons on the whole would have to have very vigorous rehabilitation programs before the idea had any justice in it. If an indeterminate sentence is too extreme, let us ask some hard questions and make some changes. Things are not right now.

The current status of the insanity plea is another area where the authors think that authority is letting society down. Legal records are replete with cases in which "expert" witnesses of different philosophical bents nitpick on the witness stand about whether the defendant should go to a mental hospital or to a jail.

In our experience the mental health system is generally asked to do much more than it reasonably can do. Most often it is overloaded. Even if it were not overloaded, its ability to change behavior is in actuality a lot less than most people realize. Much of this misunderstanding is the fault of the mental health profession itself, which has oversold its ability. The authors are mental health professionals with considerable experience in a wide variety of settings. They are quite adept at defining or diagnosing a problem. Doing something about it, given the resistance to change of the formed human character, is quite another matter. In an hour or two a social worker can often see the central conflict in a human dilemma. Ten years later that social worker may still be struggling, still trying to effect some change in that central conflict. The difference between recognizing the problem and doing something about it is often as marked as night and day. Yet these distinctions are frequently overlooked when loosely talking about treatment or rehabilitation.

If this is the situation, why is so much effort spent in trying to decide which of two bleak alternatives, the corrections system or the mental health system, is most appropriate in a given case? Why waste precious resources in making such a decision?

We would like to see an alternative to the insanity plea, specifically that the court be allowed to decide whether the defendant committed the act or not. If the act is such that the defendant constitutes a danger to society, then the defendant should be kept in custody at some institution. Whether this institution is called a prison or a hospital really is not that significant. It is suspected that the average hospital for the criminally insane does not provide much more treatment than some prisons do anyway.

This institution should have a number of different parts. One part might be for those people who are quite irrational and schizophrenic. Another part might be for the calculating psychopath.

Again there are many arguments against doing away with the insanity plea. In theory they have some merit. But if one looks at how the system is actually working, theory becomes less relevant. Changes of some sort have to be made.

We do not like to be alarmists, but at times we *are* alarmed when we see so many people who adopt an extreme right or left position. The less responsible the existing authority is, the more chance of success these frightening extremists have. Authority has to be continually facing those areas of its inadequacies in a brutally honest way.

Ponder again that profound line, "The public are the police, and the police are the public."

Questions for Discussion

1. How is authority obtained?
2. What do you think about the indeterminate sentence?
3. Is the insanity plea necessary for our criminal justice system to be equitable?

INDEX